UNDERSTANDING AI

ANTISOCIAL PERSONALITY DISORDER:

Criminals, Chemical Abusers, and Batterers

By Gregory L. Little, ED.D.
& Kenneth D. Robinson, ED.D.

EAGLE WING BOOKS, INC.

Understanding And Treating Antisocial Personality Disorder: Criminals, Chemical Abusers, and Batterers

Table of Contents

"There is a purpose to psychiatric diagnosis. It is to enable mental health professionals to...communicate with each other..., comprehend the pathological processes..., and control psychiatric outcomes."
Robert Spitzer (1975) DSM-III

The need for a classification of mental disorders has been clear throughout the history of medicine...
DSM — IV (1994)

INTRODUCTION

One of the most problematical and misunderstood issues in treating substance abuse is the remarkably large proportion of abusers with a coexisting Personality Disorder (PD). Treatments for PDs have always been viewed as rather ineffective and, when a PD co-exists with a substance abuse problem, treatment effectiveness becomes even more tenuous. In addition, substance abusers with PDs are likely to be viewed and managed inconsistently by treatment professionals (MacKay, 1986). This is due, in part, to vast differences in training and varying treatment philosophy often seen in chemical dependency specialists. For example, the authors have observed countless counselors who insist that chemical abuse causes what "appears to be" antisocial personality disorder. If the chemical abuse is successfully treated, their reasoning goes, the antisocial personality disorder will disappear.

Personality Disorders are considered by many professionals to be the most researched of all psychological and psychiatric diagnoses (Gunderson, 1983; Hilsenroth, Hibbard, Nash, & Handler, 1993; Widiger, Frances, Spitzer, & Williams, 1988). In view of the substantial body of literature on PDs, it is surprising that many who treat substance abusers with coexisting PDs attempt to treat the substance abuse as a separate problem in the belief that substance abuse causes antisocial behavior or that the antisocial behavior will cease when substance abuse ceases. In addition, it is also remarkable that inappropriate counseling and treatment methods continue to be applied to antisocial abusers in the belief or hope that antisocial abusers will respond favorably to traditional mental health, educational, and other counseling interventions. Many counselors still persist in using client-centered counseling approaches with offenders believing that helping the offenders understand their feelings will somehow reduce offending. With a few notable exceptions, it is well documented and accepted that almost all therapeutic interventions with antisocial substance abusers fail to reduce their substance abuse or antisocial behavior. However, during the past decade, treatment interventions have been devised, tested, and researched indicating that some substance abusers with Antisocial Personality Disorder (ASPD) can successfully be treated leading to significant declines in both substance abuse and antisocial behavior. In particular, cognitive-behavioral and behavioristic-oriented approaches have been effective with ASPD abusers because they attempt to treat the core issues of ASPD rather than its associated symptoms (e.g. substance use and abuse). Thus, effective interventions for the ASPD client must take into account the unique personality

Personality Disorders are considered by many professionals to be the most researched of all psychological and psychiatric diagnoses.

characteristics and defense mechanisms displayed by these clients while motivating and facilitating clients to change. Understanding the dynamics and thought processes of ASPD clients is an essential component for successful treatment of the symptoms of ASPD. This monograph serves as an introduction to the history and development of treatments for ASPD and provides current insights and developments in effectively treating ASPD.

Background & History

Many substance abuse professionals inappropriately tend to view ASPD as synonymous with criminal behavior and "criminal personality." Although the large majority of criminals are diagnosable with ASPD, not all are. Likewise, many of those with ASPD are not criminals but do share certain traits and behavioral patterns with other ASPDs. In addition, most substance abusers and about half of all alcoholics who enter treatment are also diagnosable as having ASPD or one of its associated personality disorders. Programs, however, are hesitant to label their clients with the diagnosis. (This may be due, in part, to the long-standing tradition of third party payers denying claims with ASPD as the primary diagnosis.) Thus, there is a great overlap between substance abuse, alcoholism, and ASPD that has long been recognized and studied.

Genesis Of The Terms Psychopath & Sociopath

In the 18th and 19th centuries, early clinicians like Pinel and Rush speculated that criminal conduct, immoral behavior, drug use, and alcoholism were forms of mental illness. In 1835, the term *"moral insanity"* was first used by psychiatrist J. C. Prichard to describe "perverted or depraved" behavior stemming from a mental derangement without apparent intellectual problems. In the late 1800s the term *"psychopath"* was applied to such persons because it was believed that a hereditary influence caused the disorder (Davidson, 1956). In the 20th century, the term *"sociopath"* was increasingly used (Overholser & Owens, 1961) because of two factors. The first factor was that the sociopath aimed his or her behavior against society's laws and mores. Secondly, it was believed that social conditions played a large part in the development of sociopathic behavior (Bootzin & Acocella, 1984). Partridge (1930) introduced the term *sociopath.*

When psychological diagnosis was revised in 1952, ASPD was placed under sociopathic personality disturbances in support of the recognition of the role of society in its development. The sociopathic personality in the diagnostic revision of 1952 had a number of related subgroups including alcoholism, drug addiction, and other dyssocial and antisocial reactions.

Despite the lack of understanding and controversy surrounding its causes, sociopathic behavior was absorbed into psychopathology as a "character" or "personality" disorder. At the same time, there was agreement that alcoholism, drug addiction, and sociopathic behavior were related disorders. Later, the PDs and substance abuse disorders were separated, although it was recognized that many of those with PDs had substance abuse problems and many substance abusers had PDs. Character and personality disorders are not typically considered to be "diseases," an illness, or a psychosis. They are inappropriate, dysfunctional behavioral patterns and personality styles. In 1957 the *American Psychiatric Association's Psychiatric Glossary* defined the psychopath as:

> "a person whose behavior is predominantly amoral or antisocial and characterized by impulsive, irresponsible actions satisfying only immediate and narcissistic interests without concern for obvious and implicit social consequences, accompanied by minimal outward evidence of anxiety or guilt."

Therefore, the habitual criminal was considered a type of sociopath just like many alcoholics and drug addicts since their antisocial behavior affected many others. This categorization has always been found to have limited usefulness. As a result, efforts to better diagnose sociopaths continued. At the same time, an effort to separate alcoholism and substance dependence from personality and character disorders occurred.

The first *Diagnostic and Statistical Manual* of the American Psychiatric Association (*DSM*) in 1960 began to divide sociopaths into two categories and placed substance abuse diagnoses into Axis I. The DSM-III later divided antisocials into two categories: 1) those who have had an enduring pattern of antisocial behavior from childhood or adolescence, and, 2) those who appear to have begun antisocial behavior in adulthood (after age 18) (Bootzin & Acocella, 1984).

Today, the term *psychopath* is used predominantly from a psychodynamic viewpoint. Persons labelled psychopathic are typically considered "mean, criminal, manipulative, or sometimes entrepreneurial" — a practice that has lead to misunderstanding and treatment ineffectiveness (Reid, 1985). Myers' introductory text, *Psychology* (1992), cites extreme ASPDs (e.g., Charles Manson) as clever con artists or serial killers, while many other criminals (who are clearly antisocial) do not fit the extremes. The term sociopath is still used by some sociologists and criminologists. In common or popular usage, both the terms (psychopath and sociopath) are often thought to be the severest forms of criminal personalities. It is a common practice to view sociopaths and psychopaths as existing on a continuum from mild, to moderate, to extreme and to term their disorder ASPD.

That ASPDs create huge problems for society is unquestionable. The costs to society in crime, effects on victims, incarceration and apprehension, health costs of victims, families, and the perpetrator, substance abuser, and alcoholic is staggering. *The Comprehensive Textbook of Psychiatry* (Freedman, Kaplan, & Sadock, 1976) states that sociopaths comprise a small but quite costly segment of society because their behavior requires disproportionate attention. From costly efforts to control and manage their childhood problems to criminal justice costs and added costs to society in taking care of their victims and their deserted families, society pays a disproportionate share because of ASPDs (p. 1287).

CHARACTERISTICS OF
THE ANTISOCIAL PERSONALITY

The textbook *Psychopathology* (Page, 1971) described ASPD as a diagnosis..."loosely applied to a heterogeneous group of individuals whose life style is marked by the immediate gratification of impulses and egocentric desires without regard or concern for the feelings and welfare of others" (p. 317). Page divided the pathological behavior of antisocials into three areas: "...sociopaths may engage in unethical, immoral, or criminal behavior" (p. 317)

Page (1971) summarizes those with ASPD as a diverse group: "They have no sense of loyalty or responsibility...Other people are regarded as dupes or suckers, to be used and exploited. Successful (ASPDs) may be quite charming, persuasive, and socially adroit. When caught in some misdeed, they may skillfully extricate themselves by lying, blaming others (including the victim), begging forgiveness, and making a show of remorse. The true sociopath, however, does not experience genuine anxiety, guilt, or remorse for the anguish and suffering he causes others. Punishment has no deterrent effect. All that is learned from past experience is to be more circumspect next time" (p. 317). Page also cites impulsiveness, low frustration tolerance, lack of empathy, thrill seeking, and egocentricity as typical common characteristics in the ASPD.

Noyes' Modern Clinical Psychiatry (Kolb, 1968) cites the ASPDs' often irritable, arrogant, and unyielding attitudes and behavior going on to say that they are rarely genuinely remorseful. "Frequently they show a rebellious attitude toward authority and society....They are cynical, devoid of a sense of honor or of shame, and are lacking in sympathy, affection, gratitude, or other social and esthetic sentiments ....Many take pleasure in their struggle with the law and feel pride in their accomplishments... Punishments

> *...sociopaths may engage in unethical, immoral, or criminal behavior... The true sociopath however, does not experience genuine anxiety, guilt, or remorse for the anguish and suffering he causes others. ... They are incapable of maintaining satisfying relationships.*

Antisocials do not experience deep emotions but have great ability to pick apart feelings. ... and often display extreme emotional outbursts to gain sympathy and impress observers. ... The disorder begins in childhood or adolescence and tends to affect many areas in their lives.

are considered as expressions of injustice and have no deterrent effect" (p. 505). Kolb's text additionally states that the ASPD will conveniently forget events ("profess amnesia"), and often display extreme emotional outbursts to gain sympathy and impress observers (p. 506).

Freedman, et. al. (1975) stated that antisocials tend to care about satisfying only their immediate needs and that they are characterized by hedonism and narcissism. They are incapable of maintaining meaningful relationships. Antisocials do not experience deep emotions but have great ability to pick apart feelings. Antisocials understand shame and guilt but don't actually experience them. The disorder begins in childhood or adolescence and tends to affect many areas in their lives.

More modern textbooks amplify earlier statements regarding ASPD: "the person (with ASPD) is typically a male whose lack of conscience becomes plain before age 15, as he begins to lie, steal, fight, or display unrestrained sexual behavior. In adulthood, he may be unable to keep a job, be irresponsible as a spouse and parent, and be assaultive or otherwise criminal. When the antisocial personality combines a keen intelligence with amorality, the result may be a clever con artist...; antisocial personalities feel little and fear little." (David Myers' *Psychology*, 1992; p. 471).

The DSM-II summarized ASPDs thusly: "They are incapable of significant loyalty to individuals, groups, or social values. They are grossly selfish, callous, irresponsible, impulsive, and unable to feel guilt or to learn from experience or punishment. Frustration tolerance is low. They tend to blame others or offer plausible rationalization for their behavior."

In his classic book, *Deviant Children Grown Up: A Sociological and Psychiatric Study of Sociopathic Personality* (1966), L. N. Robbins outlined the most common symptoms during childhood predictive of adult ASPD. Much of this classic research that follows has been employed in formulating the diagnostic criteria for the disorder. The number following the symptom is the percent of ASPD diagnosed adults who had the symptom during their childhood:

Theft (83%)
Incorrigibility (80%)
Truancy (66%)
Running away from home (65%)
Negative peers as companions (56%)
Physically aggressive (45%)
Impulsive (38%)
Reckless behavior (35%)
Irresponsible behavior (35%)
Slovenly appearance (32%)
Bedwetting (32%)
Lack of guilt (32%)
Pathological lying (26%)
Sexual perversions (18%)

Robbins' classic work went on to tabulate the most common symptoms of adult antisocials. The number following the symptom is the percent of those with ASPD who have a significant problem in the respective life area:

Alcohol/Drug Abuse (90%)
Problems with work (85%)
Marital problems (81%)
Financially dependent (79%)
Arrests (75%)
School/educational problems (71%)
Impulsive behavior (67%)
Sexual behavior (64%)
Vagrancy (60%)
Belligerence (58%)
Social isolation (56%)
Lack of guilt (40%)
Somatic complaints (31%)
Use of aliases (29%)
Pathological lying (16%)
Suicide attempts (11%)

It should be noted that *the connection between substance abuse and alcoholism has long been apparent in ASPDs.* Robbins' (1966) study found that about 90% of ASPDs displayed such difficulties. These findings have also been verified in more recent times and are discussed elsewhere.

Researchers have found that ASPDs tend to display consistent, *enduring* personality characteristics. While not all of those with the disorder display all of the common characteristics, there is a consistent *core* of traits usually found. Treatment professionals often expect to see the extremes of ASPD personality traits in antisocial clients, however, in actuality each of the common traits can vary from mild to extreme. This can cause some confusion for some treatment providers, especially those who work almost exclusively in settings likely to house large numbers of ASPDs. For example, many counselors who work in prison settings often come to view offenders with mild ASPD characteristics as *not* having ASPD because other offenders with extreme ASPD characteristics are observed in such a stark contrast. It is appropriate to view ASPD on a graduated scale like a thermometer ranging from mild ASPD to extreme ASPD. Bursten (1972) characterized the more common personality traits of ASPDs as:

Manipulative
Selfish
Egocentric
Callous
Irresponsible
Impulsive
Lack of Guilt
Lack of Genuine Remorse
Fail to Learn From Experience
Fail to Learn From Punishment
Have Low Frustration Tolerance
Blame Others or Society for Their Problems
Make Excuses
Have Superficial Relationships
Produce Conflict With Their Behavior

Probably the most respected and seminal work in studying ASPDs was Hervey Cleckley's *The Mask of Sanity* (1964). Cleckley's description is probably the most cited classic work even today, and almost every research study on ASPD has verified his profile of the antisocial personality. In his book, Cleckley listed the basic clinical profile of the ASPD:

> *Superficial charm and apparent "intelligence"*
> *Not delusional or clinically irrational*
> *Unreliable*
> *Insincere and untruthful*
> *Lack of shame*
> *Lack of remorse*
> *Antisocial behavior occurs without appropriate
>   motivation*
> *Poor judgement*
> *Failure to profit from experience*
> *Egocentric*
> *Lack of ability to love*
> *Restricted repertoire of feelings*
> *Lack and loss of insight*
> *Lack of appropriate interpersonal responses*
> *Acts out under the influence*
> *Capable of acting out while sober*
> *May attempt suicide but rarely carries out*
> *Impersonal sex life*
> *Has no life plan*

Characteristics of the Antisocial Personality

In his classic book *Deviant Children Grown Up: A Sociological and Psychiatric Study of Personality* (1966), L.N. Robbins outlined the most common symptoms during childhood predictive of adult APD. The number following the symptom is the percent of adults with APD who had the symptoms during childhood:

Theft (83%)

Incorrigibility (80%)

Truancy (66%)

Running away from home (65%)

Negative peers as companions (56%)

Physically aggressive (45%)

Impulsive (38%)

Reckless behavior (35%)

Irresponsible behavior (35%)

Slovenly appearance (32%)

Bedwetting (32%)

Lack of guilt (32%)

Pathological lying (26%)

Sexual perversions (18%)

Robbins' classic work went on to tabulate the most common symptoms of adult antisocials. The number following the symptom is the percent of those with APD who have a significant problem in the respective life area:

Alcohol/Drug Abuse (90%)
Incorrigibility (80%)
Problems with work (85%)
Running away from home (65%)
Marital problems (81%)
Physically aggressive (45%)
Financially dependent (79%)
Reckless behavior (35%)
Arrests (75%)
Slovenly appearance (32%)
School/education problems (71%)
Lack of guilt (32%)
Impulsive behavior (67%)
Sexual behavior (64%)
Vagrancy (60%)
Belligerence (58%)
Social isolation (56%)
Lack of guilt (40%)
Somatic complaints (31%)
Use of aliases (29%
Pathological lying (16%)
Suicide attempts (11%)

Bursten (1972) characterized the more common personality traits of APDs as:

Manipulative

Selfish

Egocentric

Callous

Irresponsible

Impulsive

Lack of Guilt

Lack of Genuine Remorse

Fail to Learn From Experience

Fail to Learn From Punishment

Have Low Frustration Tolerance

**Blame Others or Society
for Their Problems**

Make Excuses

Have Superficial Relationships

**Produce Conflict
With Their Behavior**

Hervey Cleckley's *The Mask of Sanity* (1964) description of ASPD is perhaps the most important research study on ASPD. Almost every study on ASPD has verified his profile of the Antisocial Personality. Cleckly listed the basis clinical profile of ASPD as:

Superficial charm and appears 'intelligent'

Not delusional or clinically irrational

Unreliable

Insincere and untruthful

Lack of shame

Lack of remorse

Antisocial behavior occurs without appropriate motivation

Poor judgement

Failure to profit from experience

Egocentric

Lack of ability to love

Restricted repertoire of feelings

Lack and loss of insight

Lack of appropriate interpersonal responses

Acts out under the influence

Capable of acting out while sober

May attempt suicide but rarely carries out

Impersonal sex life

Has no life plan

DSM-IV DIAGNOSTIC CRITERIA FOR ASPD

The *DSM-IV* section on Personality Disorders codes PDs on Axis II. The criteria for ASPD refer to "behaviors or traits that are characteristic of the person's recent past (usually the past year) and long-term functioning (generally since adolescence or early adulthood). The *DSM-IV* is careful to state that ASPD represents a pattern of behavior over time showing that the person disregards other's rights. In addition, even the *DSM-IV* notes that ASPD is sometimes referred to as psychopathy, sociopathy, or dyssocial disorder. Also noted is that deceit and manipulation are core elements of the disorder. *ASPD is an Axis II, Cluster B disorder*, associated with the other Cluster B disorders: Borderline Personality Disorder, Histrionic Personality Disorder, and Narcissistic Personality Disorder. These other Cluster B disorders are briefly discussed later.

The diagnosis of ASPD requires that four separate characteristics be present in the client. The four criteria are paraphrased here from the *DSM-IV*. Readers are encouraged to refer to the *DSM-IV* for the exact wording. According to the *DSM-IV*, the four necessary diagnostic criteria are: 1) That the client be 18 years of age at the time of diagnosis; 2) That some evidence of Conduct Disorder be present with its onset before age 15; 3) That a pattern of irresponsible and antisocial behavior have occurred since age 15; and, 4) That the antisocial behavior occur at times other than during diagnosable Schizophrenia or Manic Episodes.

> **1) That the client be 18 years of age at the time of diagnosis; 2) That some evidence of Conduct Disorder be present with its onset before age 15; 3) That a pattern of irresponsible and antisocial behavior have occurred since age 15; and, 4) That the antisocial behavior occur at times other than during diagnosable Schizophrenia or Manic Episodes.**

1. Client Age

Since ASPD is a chronic, ongoing pattern of antisocial behavior since adolescence, the diagnosis requires that the client be at least age 18. Prior to age 18, clients displaying antisocial behavior are typically diagnosed as having Conduct Disorder or one of its related diagnoses. The related diagnoses include Oppositional Disorder or Attention Deficit-Hyperactivity. Note that unusually early chemical use, including smoking, is one of the diagnostic criteria for Conduct Disorder.

2. Evidence of Conduct Disorder Behavior Prior to Age 15 (only need three of the following before age 15 to qualify):

Many ASPDs were not diagnosed as having Conduct Disorder in their childhoods and the actual diagnosis is not necessary for the diagnosis of ASPD to be made. Evidence of some aspects of Conduct Disorder is necessary. Some clinicians believe that in some cases lack of apparent childhood problems may be because of various factors that allowed the individual to escape detection. Some adolescents can also occasionally be raised in surroundings that approve of childhood antisocial behaviors. In general, clinicians ask adult clients a series of questions designed to uncover whether antisocial behaviors were present in their adolescence. Conduct Disorder will be addressed again, however, evidence of Conduct Disorder can be found if some of the following behaviors were present before age 15: fights, incidences of bullying, using a weapon, cruelty to animals or people, forcing sexual activity, theft or stealing, arson, repetitive vandalism, shoplifting, frequent deceit and lying, and problems at school or violating reasonable parental rules. In general, the behaviors must have caused some sort of problems in school, work, or social life.

3. Pattern of Antisocial Behavior Since Age 15 (must have only three or more of the following seven items to qualify):

1. A repeating pattern of performance of unlawful behaviors for which the individual could be arrested.

2. A pattern of lying and deceit. Use of aliases (false names). Using lies and manipulation to achieve money, pleasure, or other advantages.

3. A pattern of impulsive actions including quitting jobs suddenly, traveling with no itinerary, moving and having no current

address, or rapidly ending and starting new relationships.

 4. A pattern of physical aggressiveness including fighting and assaults.

 5. Lack of concern for other's safety or welfare including any of the following: child neglect/abuse, high-risk sexual behavior, thrill-seeking behaviors, driving while intoxicated, reckless driving, putting others at risk, or similar risky behaviors.

 6. A pattern of irresponsibility regarding work, paying bills, or following through with important responsibilities. Periods of unemployment, job abandonment, failure to pay family support, or defaulting on debts or obligations are examples.

 7. Lack of remorse or indifference to those the person hurt. Making excuses, blaming the victim, minimizing harm, and failure to make amends are all examples.

4. The antisocial behavior occurs at times when the person is not actively Schizophrenic or in a diagnosable Manic Episode.

 This does not mean that a person with diagnosable schizophrenia or mania can't also be diagnosed with ASPD. Some schizophrenics who have their psychotic symptoms under control through the use of medication can display ASPD. However, in the course of active, untreated schizophrenia, some schizophrenics can perform acts that appear to be antisocial. Active mania can also lead to antisocial behavior. The issue that clinicians look to uncover with such patients is what the schizophrenic or manic does when their symptoms are under control with medication.

RELATED PERSONALITY DISORDERS

 Several other Cluster B Personality Disorders are frequently seen in substance abuse treatment. Borderline PD, Histrionic PD, and Narcissistic PD are often encountered. While each is diagnostically viewed as a separate, distinct category, it is also clear that they are a related cluster. In a recent paper reviewing research on *DSM-III-R* PDs (Jovanovic, Svrakic, & Tosevski, 1993), the relationship was made clear: "...*many PDs, classified as separate nosologic units, reflect different behavioral expression of the same personality deviation or co-occurring endpoints of the same pathogenesis"* (p. 559).

Borderline PD

BPD is characterized by unstable and rapidly changing patterns of mood, relationships, self-image and identity. It typically begins by early adulthood. Behaviors frequently seen (requires five of the following) include unstable and intense relationships where rapid alterations between feelings of overidealization and rejection occur; impulsive, potentially self-damaging behavior such as binge eating, dangerous driving, spending, and substance use; rapid and wide shifts in mood including sudden depression, irritability, or anxiety; frequent anger displays, uncontrollable temper, fights; self-mutilation, suicidal threats or gestures; identity disturbances and uncertainty including sexual orientation, goals, careers, friends; chronic boredom and emptiness; frantic behavior avoiding real (or perceived) abandonment.

Histrionic PD

HPD also typically begins by early adulthood and is characterized by extremes of emotion and attention-seeking behavior with four or more characteristics: Included are demands for approval or praise; inappropriate seductive appearance; over concern with physical appearance; exaggeration of emotion; uncomfortable when not the center of attention; shows rapid shifts in emotion; self-centered, no ability to delay gratification; talks in generalities without giving details.

Narcissistic PD

NPD, as do the other Cluster B disorders, begins by early adulthood. It is characterized by grandiosity, hypersensitivity, egocentricity, and lack of empathy with five or more of the following: shows humiliation, shame, or anger when criticized; exploits others; has exaggerated sense of importance, wants to be seen as special without achievement; says problems are unique or special; has frequent fantasy of success (including love); feels entitled beyond others; seeks constant attention, wants to be admired; has little or no empathy; is often envious.

Other Diagnostic Issues

DSM criteria for ASPD have come under frequent attack for being too cumbersome and focusing too strongly on antisocial behavior rather than the personality traits associated with the disorder (Hare, Hart, & Harpur, 1991). The APA's task force on updating the *DSM-III-R* to the *DSM-IV* altered some of the ASPD criteria in an effort to simplify the disorder's criteria. Others have attempted to further simplify ASPD by making the diagnosis easier to uncover through the use of questionnaires. It is probable that shortened forms of the current ASPD criteria will be adapted or one of the commercially available checklists for the disorder will be more widely used. Those who make decisions regarding the supervision status of offenders are especially interested in utilizing such checklists to predict suitability for various sanctions. In general, all of these shortened forms and checklists incorporate the current concepts of ASPD into their diagnostic procedures. For example, the *ICD-10* criteria for *Dyssocial Personality Disorder* has seven items paraphrased and shortened below:

1. Lack of empathy and callous concern for others.
2. Irresponsible behavior and disregard for rules and norms.
3. Inability to have sustained relationships.
4. Low frustration tolerance.
5. Lack of guilt and inability to learn from experience.
6. Blames others and rationalizes behavior when in conflict.
7. Irritability.

The Hare Psychopathy Checklist, another scale used for diagnosing ASPD and predicting behavior, has 10 items. These include: superficiality and glibness, overly high self-appraisal, lack of remorse and empathy, deceit and manipulation, adult and adolescent behavior problems, impulsivity, and irresponsibility (Hare, 1980).

One of the most difficult issues some substance abuse counselors fail to understand is how ASPD can be diagnosed when the client has a substance abuse problem. Substance abuse, to many chemical dependency counselors, is a cause of antisocial behavior. Quite frankly, there is little empirical evidence to support that belief. This issue will be discussed later in this monograph. However, we hasten to point out that many substance abusers and alcoholics do not display antisocial behavior. Chemical abusers who do display antisocial behavior may also be diagnosed as having ASPD, especially if there is any evidence that they performed certain antisocial acts before their chemical abuse or at times when they aren't using drugs. Research has shown that the use of certain drugs or alcohol accelerates antisocial behavior, but it does not appear to be the causal factor.

CONDUCT DISORDER, ASPD, & DRUG USE

Adult ASPD is usually preceded by a distinct set and pattern of antisocial behaviors during late childhood and adolescence. A key word here is *pattern*. Research has shown that most males (90% to 94%) and most females (65% to 90%) have committed at least *one* delinquent act prior to age 18 (Snyder & Sickmund, 1995; p. 49 for a review). However, the same research has shown that about 30% of males and less than 10% of females had performed *three* delinquent acts by their 18th year of age. Thus, it is true that most adolescents normally engage in some delinquent behavior, however, far fewer engage in a pattern of delinquent behavior. The *DSM-IV* states that the range of incidence of conduct disorder in males is 6% to 16% with urban areas showing a higher level. The range for females is 2% to 9%. Symptoms of conduct disorder are often seen in children as young as 6 years old, however, by age 16, those who have conduct disorder will have displayed its characteristic pattern of unconcern for other's rights and property and deceit/manipulation.

One observation consistently made about children and adolescents that display conduct disorder symptoms is that they also tend to abuse drugs/alcohol. In recent years a substantial amount of research has been conducted on this observation. Van Kamen & Loeber (1994), for example, evaluated the relationship between drug use and crime in 506 urban males. Their results showed that property crime patterns *preceded* drug usage. As the youth then began using drugs, their pattern and severity of crime tended to escalate. Research sponsored by the National Institute of Drug Abuse (Swan, 1993) has shown the same. NIDA research has indicated that "conduct disorder is in large part the common forerunner of both drug abuse and criminality, challenging the assumption that drug use causes crime" (p. 6).

THE INCIDENCE OF ANTISOCIAL PERSONALITY DISORDER

Early research estimated the incidence of ASPD at between 1% to up to 15% of the population depending upon the region, locale, and demographics (see Freedman, et. al., 1976 for a review). Rosenthal (1970) reviewed research on the prevalence of ASPD and cited data estimating that between .05% to 15% of the population had the disorder. The DSMs have consistently placed the incidence of ASPD at around 3% of the adult population with men out numbering women about eight to one. Robins and Regier's (1991) major study conducted in the early 1990s, showed that 2.6% of the non-institutionalized population was diagnosable as having ASPD. Of non-institutionalized men, 4.5% were diagnosable as having ASPD while noninstitutionalized women showed a rate of 0.8%. Among racial groupings, Robins and Regier found 2.3% of Blacks, 2.6% of Whites, and 3.4% of Hispanics were diagnosable as having ASPD.

It should be noted that all of the research conducted on the incidence of ASPD and other disorders has been conducted on non-institutionalized populations. Thus, the actual incidence of ASPD in the entire population would be somewhat higher. For example, in 1990, 1,118,000 offenders were incarcerated during the time of Robins and Regier's study. As will be discussed later, about 80% of those incarcerated have ASPD. Thus, in 1990 the actual incidence of ASPD in the entire adult population would be closer to 3%.

The most recent and probably most accurate demographic data ever collected on the incidence of ASPD was published in January 1994 in the *Archives of General Psychiatry* (Kessler, McGonagle, Zhao, Nelson, Hughes, Eshleman, Whittchen, & Kendler, 1994). In this study, the first of its kind, the prevalence of all *DSM-III-R* diagnoses in the adult, noninstitutionalized population was collected by interviewers from all 48 states from over 8,000 subjects. Conducted as the *National Comorbidity Survey*, the Kessler, et. al. study is considered to be one of the most accurate of all such studies. This study showed that 5.8% of male adults had ASPD while 1.2% of females had ASPD. Overall, 3.5% of the population had ASPD. With institutionalized ASPDs added to the totals, it can reliably be estimated that 3.7% to 4% of the population has ASPD.

SUBSTANCE ABUSE, OFFENDERS, AND ASPD

The 1994 *National Comorbidity Survey* described in the prior section also addressed rates of alcoholism and substance dependence. That survey showed that in the last 12 months, 2.8% of the population was dependent on drugs while 7.2% was dependent on alcohol. In The *Chemically Dependent Criminal Offender* (1993), relapse prevention specialist Terrence Gorski cites reliable figures indicating that 100% of the incarcerated prisoner population are drug and / or alcohol users and that 70% have serious (dependency) problems with drugs and alcohol. Gorski also cites figures stating that *nearly 100% of incarcerated offenders have ASPD or another related Personality Disorder*. Gorski and others view ASPD as a "criminal personality" that overlaps with chemical abuse. Substantial research has been conducted on the DSM criteria applied to offender populations. Virtually all research tends to yield figures citing that between 76% (Hare, 1980) to 80% (Guze, Goodwin, & Crane, 1969) of all offenders have ASPD. Hare, et. al. (1991) cite research indicating that in 1990, the Correctional Service of Canada found that 75% of all male adults incarcerated in Canada had ASPD. It may be wise to state that the other 20% or so of offenders that are *not* ASPD diagnosable, are not

Percentage of adult population with substance abuse diagnoses. Source — National Comorbidity Study. Reprinted from Psychopharmacology (Little, 1997)						
	Males		Females		Total	
	12-months	Lifetime	12-months	Lifetime	12-months	Lifetime
Drug Abuse	1.3	5.4	0.3	3.5	0.8	4.4
Drug Dependence	3.8	9.2	1.9	5.9	2.8	7.5
Alcohol Abuse	3.4	12.5	1.6	6.4	2.5	9.4
Alcohol Dependence	10.7	20.1	3.7	8.2	7.2	14.1
All Substance Abuse Diagnoses Combined	16.1	35.4	6.6	17.9	11.3	26.6

often without a diagnosis. Depression, retardation, other PDs, and various psychoses comprise the diagnoses in the bulk of the remaining offenders.

With the advent of drug testing utilizing urinalysis and hair analysis, the extent of substance abuse in offenders is becoming more apparent. The incidence of substance abuse among arrestees is astonishing. "Voluntary surveys have shown that about 35% of inmates admit to being under the influence of drugs at the time of their offense...*drug testing of arrestees has shown that the vast majority of those charged for crimes were positive for drugs at the time of their arrest* (Bureau of Justice Statistics, 1992a; b)" (Little & Robinson, 1994). Specifically, the 1992 Bureau of Justice urine drug testing program on arrestees (with samples taken at the time of the arrest) showed that up to 75% had cocaine in their systems at the time of their arrest. Nearly 90% were under the influence of either drugs or alcohol when arrested. Similar high drug usage rates among arrestees have continued to be reported by the Bureau of Justice. Hemphill, Hart, and Hare (1994) reported that 96% of Canadian inmates diagnosed as psychopaths using the Hare Psychopathy Checklist had substance abuse disorders (and 89% of the remaining inmates also showed substance abuse problems).

From the above research it is clear that voluntary drug or alcohol usage surveys of offenders grossly underestimate the actual incidence of drug usage. A recent study on 165 consecutive juvenile arrestees in Cleveland, Ohio showed how unreliable voluntary drug usage information from juveniles is when it is collected through intake questionnaires (Freucht, Stephens, & Walker, 1994). In their study, Freucht, et. al. found that only 7.4% of all juvenile arrestees admitted to *ever* using cocaine. Urinalysis testing indicated that 8% had cocaine metabolites in their bodies at the time of their arrest. However, the Cleveland study also performed hair analysis (the most accurate of all drug usage testing). Results showed that *60% of the arrestees had used cocaine within the last 30 days*. Thus, the voluntary drug usage information was fully eight times less than actual use when the testing information was analyzed for only the past 30 days. Magura, Kang, and Shapiro (1995) reported on a near replication of the Cleveland study with older offenders. Their study "recruited" 121 male arrestees (mean age 19 years) and found that 36% admitted to using cocaine at least once in their lives. Hair analysis showed that 67% had used cocaine in the last 30 days.

Incarcerated Offenders

The Bureau of Justice Statistics and other federal agencies routinely issue reports on inmate populations. Understanding the numbers of offenders and making comparisons to ASPD incidence can be enlightening. In 1990, for example, BJS reported that 4.3 million adults were under some sort of criminal justice supervision in the United States. That figure represented about 2.3% of the total adult population. More than half (61%) of these offenders were on probation while another 12% were on parole. About 17% were in prison while the remainder (9%) were in a jail. Thus, in 1990, only 26% of convicted offenders were incarcerated.

By 1994, 5.1 million adults were under criminal justice supervision representing 2.7% of the adult population. Probation (58%) and parole (13.5%) accounted for the majority of offenders while 19% were in prison and 9.5% were in a jail.

It should be recalled that the incidence of ASPD in the general noninstitutionalized adult population approximates 3.5% and that up to 4% or so of the total adult population has ASPD. Criminal justice "supervises" (on one level or another) about 2.7% of the adult population and it is known that the vast majority of these offenders have some degree of ASPD.

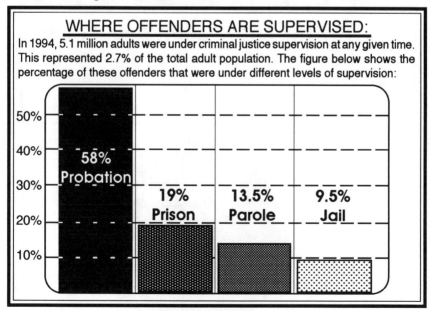

WHERE OFFENDERS ARE SUPERVISED:

In 1994, 5.1 million adults were under criminal justice supervision at any given time. This represented 2.7% of the total adult population. The figure below shows the percentage of these offenders that were under different levels of supervision:

- 58% Probation
- 19% Prison
- 13.5% Parole
- 9.5% Jail

The Most Recent Data on APD Incidence

was published in January 1994 in the *Archives of General Psychiatry. The National Comorbidity Survey*, the Kessler, et. al. study, will probably be the basis of new *DSM* data. It revealed:

5.8% of Male Adults
1.2% of Females

3.5% of Adult Population Has APD
(Figures are for noninstitutionalized adults)

For the entire adult population, the figures are probably:
3.7%

ENTIRE POPULATION

APD = 3.7%

ASPD INCIDENCE IN CHEMICAL DEPENDENCY TREATMENT PROGRAMS

Considerable evidence has been reported showing that a fairly large proportion of those entering virtually any type of treatment program for chemical dependency are diagnosable as having ASPD or a related Cluster B Personality Disorder. A 1990 study conducted in Connecticut showed that 33% of cocaine users had ASPD regardless of whether they entered treatment or not (Rounsaville & Kleber, 1985). A study of cocaine abusers in New York City who entered outpatient treatment showed that 58% had Personality Disorders (Kleinman, Miller, Millman, Woody, Todd, Kemp, & Lipton, 1990). Diagnoses of New Orleans cocaine users entering a Veterans Hospital treatment program showed that 31% had Personality Disorders (Malow, West, Williams, & Sutker, 1989).

Substantial research has been done on the personality and diagnosis of opiate and narcotic addicts entering treatment. Craig's (1993) survey reports that in all studies, about 67% of those seeking treatment for narcotic use have ASPD or a related Personality Disorder. For example, in a study of narcotic abusers in a Veteran's Hospital program in Chicago (Craig, 1988), 72% had PDs. The previously mentioned New Orleans study (Malow, et. al., 1989) found that 79% of opiate addicts had a PD. A 1992 study (Brooner, Schmidt, Felch, & Bigelow, 1992) found that 68% of inpatient and outpatient substance abusers (who had injected drugs) had ASPD. O'Boyle (1993) reported a 0.44 correlation between the multiple substance dependence and ASPD diagnoses in a group of 102 noncriminal substance abuse treatment patients who volunteered for the study. Thus, it is clear that many treatment programs that purport to treat substance abuse problems are treating clients who also have ASPD or another PD.

With regard to alcoholics, many treatment personnel have long considered alcoholism to have only a small overlap with ASPD and other personality disorders. Certainly, most treatment professionals recognize that those persons who have frequent contact with the criminal justice system because of their alcoholism are antisocial. This finding is especially recognized in multiple DWI offenders.

However, because of the nature and progression of alcoholism, many treatment programs outside of the criminal justice system have

> **Alcohol and drug abuse are seen with increased frequency among antisocials.**

failed to consider the incidence of ASPD in their populations. One such study (Hesselbrock, Meyer, & Keener, 1985), conducted in Connecticut, compared alcoholics in treatment from residential programs, the VA hospital-based programs, and a University hospital program. This study showed no major differences among client diagnoses in the three treatment sites. Results showed that 49% of the alcoholics were diagnosable with ASPD. Interestingly, this study did not include or recognize the use of alcohol and its problems with the diagnostic criteria. That is, disregarding all alcohol use and the problems associated with the alcohol use, 49% of the alcoholics in treatment programs were antisocial. Others (Penick, et. al., 1984) have found similar results in alcoholics in treatment. Consistent with these findings, the text *Psychopharmacology: Basics for Counselors* (Little, 1997) describes the three, separate modern typologies that researchers have proposed to classify alcoholics. These typologies are similar and tend to divide alcoholics into two broad categories: those with ASPD and those that don't have ASPD. Each typology defines one type of alcoholic as having the characteristics of ASPD with an early onset of alcohol use coinciding with the antisocial behavior. The alcoholic types with strong ASPD characteristics are variously termed as *Type B*, *Type II*, or *Primary ASPD with Secondary Alcoholism*. The other type of alcoholic (the non-ASPD), is apparently influenced more by environment and early-life learning.

Regarding the connection between ASPD and substance abuse, Freedman et. al. (1975) stated, "Alcohol and drug abuse are seen with increased frequency among antisocials" (p. 1293). Page (1971) also cited excessive use of alcohol and drugs common among ASPDs (p. 320) and virtually all studies on offenders have shown that 80% or more have substantial problems with chemical abuse (see Gorski, 1993). Despite such findings, many providers of substance abuse treatment continue to insist that "noncriminal" abusers in treatment are very different from the criminal abusers. Farabee, Nelson, and Spence (1993) examined this claim by comparing a group of 136 criminal justice clients referred to outpatient substance abuse treatment to 40 self-referred clients to the same facility. On

Substance Abuse and APD

The 1994 *National Comorbidity Survey* described in the text also addressed rates of alcoholism and substance dependence.

That survey showed that in the last 12 months,

2.8% of the population was dependent on drugs

7.2% was dependent on alcohol

APD and Substance Abuse Overlap

The bulk of substance dependent persons are also diagnosable as having APD. While about half of alcoholics who enter treatment also have APD, less than half of all alcoholics have APD. Almost all APDs who enter institutions or programs show some form of chemical abuse.

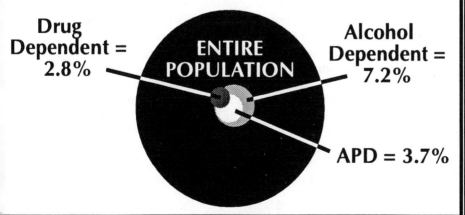

Drug Dependent = 2.8%

ENTIRE POPULATION

Alcohol Dependent = 7.2%

APD = 3.7%

seven of eleven psychological variables, the two groups were virtually identical. Criminal justice clients, however, had higher decision making scores (indicating better perceived efficacy in decision making). The noncriminal justice clients showed better ability to self assess drug problems, had more desire for help, and higher readiness for treatment.

DOES CHEMICAL ABUSE CAUSE ANTISOCIAL BEHAVIOR?

The abuse of drugs and alcohol is intimately connected to antisocial behavior. The connection is not as direct as it may seem, however, and until recently it was unclear why some drug users and alcoholics performed crime while others didn't. Psychopharmacologist Oakley Ray's (Ray & Ksir, 1990) text, *Drugs, Society, & Human Behavior*, for example, stated that research had begun clarifying the relationship between deviance and drug use. Specifically, research indicates that deviance occurs first and drug use follows the deviance. While it is true that the use of drugs can cause organic impairment in some persons, and thereby create antisocial acts, by far the majority of those performing antisocial acts while using drugs have ASPD. In the realm of criminal justice research on the relationship between drug use and crime, the findings have been clarified and solidified in that the criminal justice system has developed a firm stand.

"It is now clear that, '...research confirms the findings that crime precedes drug use and suggests that the relationship between drugs and crime is developmental rather than causal...' (Bureau of Justice Statistics, 1992b, p. 4). In short, drug use is a behavior that represents a developmental behavioral stage seen in those who are disposed to the criminal lifestyle. In 1989 we wrote that, ...'criminals would be attracted to drug use...Drug use breeds criminal behavior and criminal behavior breeds drug use' (Robinson & Little, 1989). Data indicates that criminals are attracted to the use of drugs and that the use of drugs escalates the antisocial tendencies already present in offenders. Thus, the treatment of drug use is an important and ever-present issue in dealing with offenders since a reduction in substance use would reduce antisocial behavior (but not actually cease it). However, the basic underlying issue is the antisocial personality of offenders that attracts them to both crime and drugs (Little & Robinson, 1994).

APD Incidence in Chemical Dependency Treatment Programs

Research on Personality Disorders of those in treatment programs (in both outpatient and programs) shows:

**33% to 60%
of Cocaine Abusers
have a PD or APD**

**68% to 79%
of Opiate Abusers
have APD**

**68% of
Intravenous Drug Users
have APD**

**49% of
Alcoholics
have APD**

As stated earlier, ASPD tends to develop early in life with a coinciding development of chemical abuse. The Office of Juvenile Justice and Delinquency Prevention's (Snyder & Sickmund, 1995) report on *Juvenile Offenders and Victims* states: "Researchers believe that delinquency and substance abuse are caused by the same underlying factors, rather than one causing the other" (p. 63). That report goes on to say, "drug abuse does not cause the initiation of delinquent behavior, nor delinquent behavior the initiation of drug use. However, they may have the same root causes..." (p. 63). In the field of chemical dependency treatment, it is common for workers to state that "anyone can become drug dependent" and that "alcoholics come from all walks of life." Programs typically have preprinted brochures stating that chemical abuse causes all sorts of antisocial behaviors. From one perspective, that statement is partially true. **However, chemical abuse clearly accelerates whatever antisocial tendencies the abuser already has.** There is no research showing that chemical abuse turns non-antisocials into antisocials. Thus, when a "normal" person abuses drugs (but doesn't cause organic damage to themselves), it would not be expected for them to perform antisocial acts to the extent that are are diagnosable with ASPD. *However, when criminals and those with ASPD use drugs or alcohol, **their antisocial behavior accelerates and escalates.*** In regards to drug and alcohol treatment programs, the important issues relate to effective treatment of abusers, and since antisocial abusers create enormous problems for society, effective and successful treatment of them — or incapacitation — would seem to be appropriate and necessary.

WHAT CAUSES ANTISOCIAL PERSONALITY DISORDER?

Two hundred years ago physicians and criminologists had no doubt that the criminal personality was born as such. With the advent and influence of sociology and psychology in the 20th Century, it was recognized that social conditions, environment, and upbringing played some role. Psychologists have long viewed the development of ASPD as a socialization failure (Jenkins, 1960) stemming from environment (family and social background), heredity, and physiological differences in the sociopath.

Studies have cited early maternal deprivation, separation from parents or family disintegration, rejection in the family life, and deviance on the part of parents or the primary care-givers as causative factors (see Freedman, et. al., 1976 for an overview of early research).

Introductory psychology textbooks have long recognized the influence of upbringing, inadequate reasoning, and the lack of success treating those with ASPD. *Psychology: A Dynamic Science* (Schlesinger & Groves, 1976) stated: "Apparently, the presence of a sociopathic male model is an important factor in the antisocial male's development. The sociopath's thinking is aimed at justifying his antisocial behavior by blaming others.... Because successful therapy depends upon the patient's anxiety and motivation to change, antisocial personalities are extremely difficult to treat" (p. 542).

Theories of ASPD are typically divided into Biological (Hereditary), Sociological, and Psychological orientations. For the purposes of this monograph, only a brief overview of each shall be offered (Ratliff, 1993).

Biological Theories

Biological theories have looked at genetic and hereditary consistencies in ASPDs, differences in physiological arousal levels between ASPDs and others, early-life organic damage, and differences in neurotransmitters, hormones, and other body chemicals. In general, there is data indicating that some hereditary influence is present. Mason and Frick (1994) reviewed 70 published studies on twins and adoptees and concluded, "heredity plays a significant role in the development of antisocial behavior...an average of approximately 50% of the variance in measures of antisocial behavior was accounted for by heredity. ...it is possible that our findings, which support the contention that there is an inherited predisposition to antisocial behavior, might even be an underestimate of the magnitude of the effects of heredity." In regards to Conduct Disorder, Phelps and McClintock (1994) recently reviewed the influence of heredity. They concluded that most studies show the range of hereditary influence on the development of Conduct Disorder between 24% to 90% with most studies averaging 45% to 55%. In addition, there are some significant differences in ASPDs and others in testosterone levels, serotonin levels, catecholamine, and cholesterol. For example, numerous studies point to high testosterone levels and violence, low cholesterol levels and violence, and low serotonin levels in brainstem areas of juvenile offenders. It is well known that ASPDs do not experience levels of anxiety and fear to the same extent as non-ASPDs and data from the neurochemical and body chemistry studies have tended to confirm those findings. Regarding the genetic evidence of ASPD and alcoholism, *Psychopharmacology* (Little, 1997) states:

> "A deluge of recent scientific reports have attempted to find specific genetic links to alcoholism, polysubstance abuse, and even personality disorders that are characterized by high levels of drug and alcohol use. Twin studies and the incidence of disorders across generations in families have led most researchers to believe that a genetic link must be present. Dopamine genes (including dopamine receptor genes and the dopamine reuptake transporter protein) have been found to be associated with both polydrug abuse and alcoholism (Blum, et. al., 1990; 1991; Smith, et. al., 1992). Some researchers consider the evidence overwhelming that alcoholism may be 30% to 50% or so genetically influenced with the remaining 70%-50% attributed to environmental and individual causes (Tarter, 1995), while other researchers remain skeptical (see Baron, 1993 for a brief review). Personality disorders in which those afflicted have high levels of alcoholism and/or substance abuse (e.g. Antisocial Personality Disorder) are also believed to be genetically based with up to 50% of the disorder attributed to genes (Thapar & McGuffin, 1993)."

Sociological Theories

Sociologists have offered social learning theories, social control theories, subcultural theories, and various socioeconomic explanations for ASPD. Some support for all of the theories exists. Modern sociologists have cited feelings of "socioeconomic segregation" as an explanation for how different crime rates exist in different locales. In addition, poor parenting techniques with inadequate discipline, early-life association with other poorly socialized children, and experiencing adult rejection in early life are all cited as factors.

One interesting finding that sociologists have perhaps uncovered and partially explained, is why punishment has little or no effect on ASPDs. Termed "defiance theory," it shall be presented in the treatment section.

Psychological Theories

In actuality, psychological literature and research has not uncovered a "criminal personality" as such. Rather, ASPDs and criminals tend to display a wide-range of various personality characteristics to some degree or other. This range of characteristic variables can easily lead one to simplistically conclude that criminals and ASPDs are of all types. However, if the core elements of ASPD (e.g., deception, manipulation, lack of remorse) are kept in mind, criminal justice counselors can easily surmise that ASPD exists on a continuum of severity. As to how psychological theories account for ASPD, most assert that heredity, environment, and early life experiences all play important roles. Research has uncovered several findings regarding early life influences. Early-life physical abuse, ineffective discipline, and poor relationships with parents are frequently found to be significant factors (Norden, Klein, Donaldson, Pepper, & Klein 1995). Smith and Thornberry (1995) researched the actual statistical effect on parental maltreatment on later antisocial behavior. They reported, "a history of maltreatment increases the probability of having an official (delinquency) record by .13 (e.g. 13%)".

It is interesting to note that violent criminals and those who display the extremes of ASPD tend to show high self-esteem, assertiveness, are very dogmatic, and believe they are socially desirable. In addition, they are high sensation seekers and thrill seekers. In short, research on the ASPD client shows a core of similar pathology (with variation on the degree of pathology in each personality variable).

By far, the psychological theories of ASPD are the most accepted and popular among both treatment and criminal justice specialists. Those in criminal justice do not always agree however, and many view ASPD as a nonpsychological behavioral disorder with its roots elsewhere. Those in juvenile justice are often at variance with all of the psychological, sociological, and

> *It is interesting to note that violent criminals and those who display the extremes of ASPD tend to show high self-esteem, assertiveness, are very dogmatic, and believe they are socially desirable.*

biological theories. Gibbons' *Delinquent Behavior* (1970) stated:

> "The psychogenic interpretation of delinquency has also enjoyed great popularity in the area of correctional treatment; therapeutic endeavors have often been predicated upon the assumption that the offender is a psychologically disturbed person who is in need of psychic tinkering of one kind or another. The treatment worker has often entertained an image of the juvenile offender as a defective electronic instrument which has been wired improperly or which has blown a tube. The therapy agent views his task as one of rewiring or repairing the person through some kind of psychiatric therapy....The popularity of psychogenic orientations to criminality and delinquency is certainly not due to any hard evidence....there is little convincing empirical support for the contention that delinquents are commonly plagued by emotional problems to which their deviant acts are a response....the majority of juvenile court referrals...do not appear to differ much in psychological well-being from nonoffenders." (p. 192)

TREATMENT OF ASPD
SUBSTANCE ABUSERS

The Unsuccessful Treatment of Antisocial Abusers

Prior to the mid-1980s, few professionals treating criminals or those with ASPD claimed any marked degree of success. Textbooks in corrections, criminal justice, and clinical psychology often recommended that offenders be incapacitated and held accountable for their actions and then "waited out." This was in recognition that a fairly large proportion of ASPDs simply "slow down" when they reach their late 30s and early 40s. Abusers and offenders at these ages often state, "I'm getting too old for this," or "I just can't do as much as I used to." Page's text (1971) remarked on how ASPDs' antisocial behavior progressed during adolescence, peaks in their 20s, and then tends to taper off: ASPD invariably begins before the age of 15, however, boys typically show symptoms before age 12. Its height occurs in late adolescence and early adulthood. By the time the antisocial is in his mid-40's, about 40% have shown substantial improvement.

The improvement of ASPD with age is clearly a function of age rather than therapeutic intervention. Page (1971) stated: "After the age of thirty, about a third of these patients show a moderation of overt antisocial behavior, but interpersonal relations continue to be marked by irritability and hostility...The decline in antisocial behavior appears to be mainly a function of aging" (p. 320).

> *The improvement of ASPD with age is clearly a function of age rather than therapeutic intervention. The fact that the pure psychopath has been considered an amoral person devoid of conscience and all other adjudged desirable attributes has led many to conclude, without therapeutic effort, that he is 'hopeless'.*

ASPD has long been considered untreatable by many professionals with institutions urged to incapacitate the offender until they age and become less severe and obvious sociopaths. The 1954 text, *An Introduction To Clinical Psychology* (Pennington & Berg) stated: "...for years these expressive personalities have been considered untreatable by many..." (p. 441). "The fact that the pure psychopath has been considered an amoral person devoid of conscience and all other adjudged desirable attributes has led many to conclude, without therapeutic effort, that he is 'hopeless' " (p. 443).

Page (1971) is perhaps typical in citing the lack of effective treatment for the ASPD during the decades of the 1970s and 80s.

> "The effectiveness of psychotherapy is influenced by personal distress on the part of the patient, a strong desire to change, the establishment of a warm, trusting relationship with the therapist, and mutual expectation of beneficial results. Since the sociopath sees nothing wrong with his behavior, which he finds rewarding, at least in the short run, he has no incentive to change and no interest in establishing an emotional relationship with the therapist, of which he is incapable in any case. The therapist, for his part, has been conditioned by his training and experience to regard sociopathy as incurable" (p. 321).

Literature reviews and studies tend to reveal that treatments of all kinds applied to clients with ASPD have low success rates if they are at all successful. For example, Woody, McClellan, Luborsky, & O'Brien (1985) studied treating depression, opiate addiction, and

ASPDs with some groups having overlapping diagnoses. They stated: "Antisocial personality disorder alone is a negative predictor of psychotherapy outcome." In short, the current evidence clearly shows that traditional substance abuse programming either doesn't work to change the antisocial abuser or actually makes them worse.

Summary of Outcome Research

Many chemical dependency treatment personnel are unfamiliar with the vast outcome literature on treating drug and alcohol abusing offenders. Palmer's (1993) meta-analysis on recidivism outcome studies on offenders indicates that the following approaches either don't work to reduce recidivism or actually increase it: confrontive (scared straight) approaches, vocational training, employment programs, individual counseling that is nonbehavioral in nature or psychotherapy, diversion, physical challenge, and basic education programs. In 1994, the Center for the Study and Prevention of Violence published an extensive report citing the effectiveness of various approaches for juvenile offenders (Tolan & Guerra, 1994). Among the ineffective approaches addressed in this report are psychotherapy, casework, guided group interactions, and scare programs.The authors' extensive reviews and writings on outcome literature on treating substance abusers with ASPD reveals the following:

1. No studies exist in the treatment outcome literature demonstrating that any educational programs have ever reduced subsequent antisocial behaviors by convicted drunk drivers (Foon, 1988).

2. No studies exist in the treatment outcome literature demonstrating that any traditional counseling approaches or 12-Step programs have reduced antisocial behaviors by convicted drunk drivers during the five years after their treatment (Eliny & Rush, 1992; Foon, 1988).

3. No studies exist in the treatment outcome literature showing that any form of drug education (by itself) or 12-Step (AA) based programs reduce the subsequent antisocial behavior of drug offenders (Gendreau & Ross, 1987; Lipton, Falkin, & Wexler, 1990; Little, Robinson, & Burnette, 1992).

4. No studies exist in the treatment outcome literature showing that traditional client-centered or psychodynamic therapies have reduced anti-social behavior by any offender groups (Gendreau & Ross, 1987; Lipton, Falkin, & Wexler, 1990; Little, Robinson, & Burnette, 1992).

5. About half of the outcome studies published in treatment litera-ture on educational, traditional counseling, and 12-Step programs applied to alcohol or substance abusing offenders show that treated offenders fare worse than nontreated offenders (Eliny & Rush, 1992; Foon, 1988; Gendreau & Ross, 1987; Lipton, Falkin, & Wexler, 1990; Little, Robinson, & Bur-nette, 1992).

6. Programs and approaches that do work on ASPD substance abusing clients share certain commonality and consistencies in procedures and philosophy. Therapeutic community and cognitive-behavioral inter-ventions have shown significant declines in antisocial behavior and sub-stance use by treated offenders (Bureau of Justice Statistics, 1992b; Little, Robinson, & Burnette, 1993; Little & Robinson, 1989; Little & Robinson, 1994).

Over the years, many texts have cautioned against using inappropriate treatment methodologies with offenders and those with ASPD. Freedman, et. al. (1976) stated, "...the useful-ness of outpatient psycho-therapy along traditional lines for the offender is highly questionable..." Regarding the applicability and limita-tions of Rogerian interven-tions (person-centered or cli-ent-centered therapy), Corsini's widely used text-book, *Current Psychotherapies* (1973), cautioned: "The client-centered approach is theo-retically applicable to any re-lationship where the persons want to understand each other and want to be under-

Over the years, many texts have cautioned against using inappropriate treat-ment methodologies with offenders and those with ASPD. ASPDs do not neces-sarily want to be understood. Secondly, ASPDs do not wish to open up or reveal them-selves. By their nature they are deceptive. Third, ASPDs do not want to grow for the simple reason that they do not consider themselves to be the problem.

stood; where the persons are willing to reveal themselves to some degree; and where the persons wish to enhance their own growth" (p. 153).

Within the limitations of person-centered counseling lies its weakness with ASPD. First, ASPDs do not necessarily want to be understood. Secondly, ASPDs do not wish to open up or reveal themselves. By their nature they are deceptive. Third, ASPDs do not want to grow for the simple reason that they do not consider themselves to be the problem.

Pennington and Berg's 1954 textbook, *An Introduction To Clinical Psychology*, stated the most appropriate use of Rogerian therapy: "Its most obvious area of applicability has been with college students" (p. 528). This text goes on to say, "The client-centered method has wide application to the treatment of the emotional problems of normal persons..." (p. 548).

Modern counseling texts typically state the limitations of a particular theory in a summary section. With client centered therapy, invariably it is stated that the technique has limited usefulness on antisocial clients. Despite this limitation, the tenets of client centered therapy are often cited by textbooks used in the training of substance abuse counselors as desirable, necessary, and effective counseling techniques. For example, the commonly used text, *Essentials of Chemical Dependency Counseling* (Lawson, Ellis, & Rivers, 1984), has large sections devoted to restating what the client says, reflecting back their feelings and content, developing empathy with clients, showing acceptance and reassurance of clients, and content clarification. These are, of course, the main essentials of client centered therapy. The same text nowhere cites any data indicating that the technique actually reduces substance abuse. The text *Theories and Strategies In Counseling and Psychotherapy* (Gilliland, James, & Bowman, 1994) cautions that Rogerian counseling is adequate for "healthy" clients but has problems with more disturbed clients. It recommends that the approach can be used effectively when dealing with cultural issues, coping with disabilities, and bereavement. The text cautions against using the method when clients need goal-directedness, reinforcement, short-term concrete results, and structured guidance — or when dealing with clients who have problems with mores and life styles.

Palmer (1993) has identified a list of interventions that can reduce recidivism in offender groups to a moderate degree (from 1%

to 10%). These include restitution, behavioral family intervention, behavioral counseling in groups or with individuals, and reducing supervision caseloads. Palmer identifies the most effective approaches for offenders as behavioral groups and programs, cognitive skills programs, multimodal programs including cognitive-behavioral therapy, and cognitive-behavioral therapy alone. Palmer indicates that short-term recidivism rates can be greatly reduced by such programming and that, over longer terms, recidivism can be decreased by about one-third. Tolan and Guerra (1994) echo these findings with adolescents citing behavior modification and cognitive behavioral therapy as the most effective approaches.

> *...the most effective approaches for offenders as behavioral groups and programs, cognitive skills programs, multimodal programs including cognitive-behavioral therapy, and cognitive-behavioral therapy alone.*

EFFECTIVE TREATMENT OF ANTISOCIAL ABUSERS MUST ADDRESS THESE ISSUES

Clearly, clients with ASPD must be treated in different ways than non-ASPD substance abusers for treatment to have a beneficial impact. Below is a list of specific issues that effective treatment must address.

1. Dealing With Victim's Issues and Statements.

It is certainly true that some people were victimized by their parents, schools, their military service, and by society because of prejudice and other factors. Ask yourself, *"what can I do to change these things in this client's past?"* If the answer is nothing except make them accept it and maybe feel better about it, then it's not an issue that can be treated. **Keep them focused on changing things now in an active, present-time sense.** Also remember here that many clients use victim's statements to manipulate the treatment providers and gain sympathy or shirk responsibility.

A recent study (Hindman, 1988) was conducted on offenders to assess the incidence of childhood sexual abuse. Prior to her introduction of a lie detector in the clinic, Hindman found that 67% of sex offenders reported that they were sexually victimized during their childhood. In addition, only 29% reported that they began offending during their adolescence. After the lie detector was moved into the clinic, only 21% reported they had been victimized during their childhood and 71% reported that they had begun abusing others during their childhood or adolescence. Another study (Resnick, Foy, Donahoe, & Miller, 1989) assessed the incidence of ASPD in Vietnam vets who entered treatment for Post-Traumatic Stress Disorder caused by combat exposure. While the study verified that exposure to certain types and periods of combat can produce PTSD, it was also found that pre-existing ASPD in the vets was significantly correlated to post-combat antisocial behaviors.

The implications of such research on treatment are that many ASPD clients use victim's statements as a means of subtle manipulation of treatment staff and as a means of shirking responsibility for their behavior. Thus, when programs explore the client's past with the client, the client believes that treatment staff *want* to find something to blame their current antisocial behavior upon. Such methods are counterproductive with ASPDs and are to be avoided.

2. Remember That Abusers Referred From Criminal Justice Are Not That Different From Abusers Who Were Not Referred From Criminal Justice

Data shows that many substance abusers and alcoholics are antisocial. While some chemical dependency counselors don't like to view their clients as "criminals" or as antisocial, the two groups are more similar than they might appear. Also remember that all those who have ASPD are not necessarily criminals — the two (ASPD & Criminal Personality) are not necessarily synonymous. A recent study referred to earlier (Farabee, Nelson, & Spence, 1993) compared substance abusers who entered an outpatient treatment program from criminal justice referrals to those who entered from other sources. The study compared the two groups on 11 psychosocial variables. In seven of the variables, *the two groups were virtually iden-*

tical. The criminal justice clients, however, showed *better* decision-making than the voluntary admissions. Other variables showed that the criminal justice clients see their substance abuse as *less of a problem,* they have *less desire for help* with their substance abuse behaviors, and are *less ready* for treatment. This should not be surprising since ASPDs do not view themselves as having a problem — the problem is with the system, society, or the laws.

3. Substance Abusers With ASPD Think Differently

It should be apparent at this point that ASPD clients do not see themselves as having much of a problem with drugs. Thus, it isn't surprising that they don't really want help and are "less ready for treatment." In his now classic book based on Samuel Yochelson's work with criminals, *Inside The Criminal Mind* (1984), Stanton Samenow says it bluntly: *"The essence of this approach is that criminals choose to commit crimes. Crime resides within the person and is 'caused' by the way he thinks, not by his environment. Criminals think differently from responsible people...Focusing on forces outside the criminal is futile... From regarding criminals as victims we saw that instead they were victimizers who had freely chosen their way of life... Criminals know right from wrong. In fact, some know the law better than their lawyers.* **But they believe that whatever they want to do at any given time is right for them"** (pp. xiv-xv; 10-11).

In support of this statement, research has confirmed that offenders and substance abusers show lower level of moral reasoning than others. A cognitive-behavioral approach designed by the authors (Moral Reconation Therapy®) has shown that its effectiveness is derived, in part, by raising moral reasoning. Pugh (1993) echoes this finding in his research stressing that offenders have deviant values and need approaches that "promote moral development." Spiecker (1988) identified a lack of moral emotions as a key element in ASPD clients. Others have also found that moral reasoning deficits are present in substance-abusing juvenile offenders (Morgan, Eagle, Esser, & Roth, 1993) and that relatively high moral reasoning serves as a deterrence to criminal behavior (Veneziano & Veneziano, 1992).

A simple common example of how ASPD

... relatively high moral reasoning serves as a deterrence to criminal behavior...

thinking works can be seen with many of those who are arrested for DWI and then are forced into some form of treatment. Many of the convicted drunk drivers choose to repeatedly argue with treatment personnel

> *... clients who have shown a history of violence tend to have a greater likelihood of future violence.*

that the DWI laws are unfair. It's not fair, they state repeatedly rather than choosing to look at how their behavior might have threatened others. Interestingly, the moral reasoning of convicted drunk drivers is often less than that of those convicted of felony offences (Little & Robinson, 1989).

In short, the ASPD does whatever he or she wants to do, including substance abuse, because that *is simply what they choose to do.* There is little concern for others, only themselves and their immediate gratification. Successful approaches to treat ASPDs have focused on changing how offenders think and make their decisions. Unsuccessful approaches to ASPD focus on exploring their feelings and past.

4. Understand that a Minority of ASPD Clients Are Dangerous

It is true that past behavior is often the best predictor of possible future behavior. Thus, clients who have shown a history of violence tend to have a greater likelihood of future violence. Many substance abuse counselors hesitate treating criminal substance abusers due to their fear of violence. Dealing with potentially violent ASPDs requires consistency in enforcing rules and a certainty of what is expected of them in conjunction with a certainty of the consequences of their actions. In terms of assessing a client's propensity toward dangerous violence, Tobey & Bruhn (1992) have found that the prediction of violent clients can be reliably indicated by the number of the early life memories of emotional and physical violence clients have when asked to recall the four earliest events in their lives. In general, violent clients recalled 3 or 4 severe, violent events during their childhood which typically happened at home and to them. Criminals found to be nonviolent typically recalled two or fewer such events that were less severe.

Some ASPD clients that abuse drugs and alcohol are violent — especially in their battering of those they supposedly love. A later section will address this specialized area of treatment.

5. Remember That ASPD Can Co-exist With Other Diagnoses

DSM-IV diagnosis is a mystery to many substance abuse counselors. It is probably a good idea to review the many other possible diagnoses that substance abusing clients can have. For example, studies have found that 30% to 40% of those diagnosed with Major Depression also have a Personality Disorder (see Shea, Widiger, & Klein, 1992 for a recent review of depression and PD). Also recall that studies have shown that from one third to two-thirds of those entering chemical abuse treatment probably have a Personality Disorder. Thus, treating depression will not typically do anything beneficial to ASPD symptoms. In fact, relieving depression in an ASPD client could potentially increase their antisocial behavior. This is not to say that treating depression in ASPD isn't warranted, it simply means that some other interventions must also be used.

6. Be Consistent and Firm In Enforcing Rules

ASPDs seek out and notice inconsistencies in other's behavior as justification for their own actions. It is inconceivable that treatment staff could be observed lying, drunk or under the influence, or showing favoritism toward or against certain clients and then not expect the client to do the same. When ASPDs observe staff making excuses, claiming to be victims, and focusing on their own feelings, the ASPDs' world view is reinforced. Learn to follow and enforce the rules consistently and firmly. When clients say, "rules are made to be broken," reply "rules are made to be followed."

7. Don't Engage In Philosophical Arguments About Fairness

ASPDs are experts at pointing out how unfair the world is to them and others. If they can get you to agree with them they can and will justify their actions based on the fact (which you have agreed with) that the world is unfair and must be resisted. Keep the focus on *their* situation and what is expected of them — and the consequences of their behavior. Arguing the fairness of DWI laws or drug laws with an ASPD is pointless. The simple fact is that they want to get high or drunk and don't

> *Arguing the fairness of DWI laws or drug laws with an ASPD is pointless. ...ASPDs will quickly learn to manipulate with the use of treatment terminology and jargon. ...many ASPDs do not appear to connect the behaviors they perform to the punishments they receive.*

want anyone to bother them. Fairness isn't the real issue with them — their personal pleasure is. However, the unfairness argument is part of their defense mechanisms and justification. The simple solution to this is to refuse to engage in such discussions and focus on their behavior in the program and the consequences of their behavior.

8. Refrain From The Use of Treatment Jargon

ASPDs will quickly learn to manipulate with the use of treatment terminology and jargon. *Speak in simple, common terms.* Unfortunately, clients begin to use jargon so they don't really have to discuss what is happening at a deeper level. Terminology and jargon are for professionals to more efficiently communicate with each other. If a client uses jargon, ask them exactly what it means. For example, a client might say that they agree that they minimize and justify their actions. What an ASPD means by that statement is not what a treatment professional means. They mean that the issue is trivial and they are not really going to change because they have justified their actions.

9. Understand That Punishment Does Not Effect ASPDs As It Does Others

Findings that ASPDs do not profit from experience are consistent and stem, in part, from their failure to learn from punishment. First, ASPDs do not experience fear and anxiety as non-

ASPDs do. The things "normal" people fear do not have the same effect on ASPDs. In addition, many ASPDs do not appear to connect the behaviors they perform to the punishments they receive. Instead, they blame getting caught and "unfair" rules. A recent theory (Sherman, 1993) explains how punishment can even increase crime as many studies have shown. *The Defiance Theory* postulates that the presence of four conditions leads to defiance of laws, society, and authority. These are: 1) An offender defines a punishment is unfair (whether because the laws are unjust, others get away with it, or it is established by an unjust society); 2) The offender is alienated or unattached to the community or authority issuing the punishment; 3) The offender sees the punishment as stigmatizing and rejecting them personally; 4) The offender refuses to acknowledge shame from the punishment. Thus, *stigmatizing punishments deemed unfair and inconsistent from a distant authority with which the offender has no bonds cause offenders no shame.* In fact, punishments perceived as "unfair" may actually increase the offender's rage, make him or her see society as even more unfair, view sanctions as irrelevant, and raise defiance in future behavior. Thus, sanctions on treated ASPDs must be handled in an even-handed, consistent fashion. In addition, shame, or more appropriately, the necessity and importance of shame associated with wrongful conduct must be used as a treatment tool with ASPDs.

> *Substance abuse counselors who are frustrated with clients from the criminal justice system are most likely using inappropriate treatment strategies.*

10. Use Methods Appropriate to the ASPD Client

Substance abuse counselors who are frustrated with clients from the criminal justice system are most likely using inappropriate treatment strategies. Searching the past, psychotherapy, treating adult's abuses suffered during their childhood, discussing how unfair the world is, blaming others and looking for deep-seated reasons for client behavior, and client centered approaches are all inappropriate or ineffective with ASPDs. Programs suffering high dropout rates with ASPDs are also using ineffective and inappropriate methods.

EFFECTIVE TREATMENTS FOR AN-TISOCIAL SUBSTANCE ABUSERS

A large number of outcome studies in the early 1970s found that therapeutic communities and behavioristic techniques were effective in treating Antisocial substance abusers. Freedman et. al (1976) stated "...the results of treatment within an institution using such modalities as therapeutic community and group therapy all show positive results..." (p. 1296). The authors recommend focusing therapeutic procedures that make the ASPD develop internal behavioral controls by being firm and establishing a rigid program structure. This authority/punishment-based program is easiest to establish in a housing unit or on an inpatient basis.

In treating the ASPD, Kolb's 1968 text emphasizes that once the treatment relationship is established, confrontation and pressure must be placed on the ASPD. "When the treatment relationship is established...pressure through personal and verbal behavior must be initiated...Usually such efforts must be made continuously and slowly, and infractions should be treated by withdrawal of privileges and their reinstitution on improved behavior....A sense of authority is consistently and firmly maintained.... If permissiveness is adopted for treatment of the psychopath, no focus will be established for superego growth, and, if anything, the permissiveness may aggravate the antisocial behavior" (pp. 507-508).

Over the past decade a number of specific approaches have been developed for use on offenders and antisocial clients. Some of these have proven effective while others haven't. Briefly, effective approaches with substance abusers who are antisocial can be clustered into four groupings:

1. Therapeutic Communities Using Group and Behavioristic Methods.

Early research on treating incarcerated substance abusers showed that purely behavioral management within the therapeutic community (TC) using group therapies reduced subsequent substance use and recidivism to a small, but significant, degree. The magnitude of effect was typically about an 8% reduction in reincarceration and rearrests in relative terms. The term "relative recidivism reduction" merits definition. Virtually all recidivism studies make relative comparisons. For example, if the "expected" recidivism rate is 50% (and it is reduced through programming by 10%) the new recidivism rate is 45% (10% of 50 is 5). Thus, the 8% reduction in recidivism rates seen in TCs is smaller than the 8% number seems to imply.

In modern criminal justice treatment, TCs are being touted as a means to successfully treat substance abusing offenders (Leukefeld & Tims, 1992). TCs are characterized by their clients living together in an isolated community (e.g. a specially arranged dorm) wherein all interactions are with other TC members or staff and all activities are therapeutic. Peer pressure groups are run frequently where clients hold each other accountable for behavior. A host of rules are enforced by rigid sanctions and compliant behavior is rewarded by reinforcement, increasing freedom, and moving up in a peer hierarchy. One major drawback of TCs is their large dropout rate (40-60%), the length of time necessary to accomplish meaningful change (often cited as 9-months or more), and the limited numbers who can be treated by the effort.

2. Progressively Severe Sanctions For Noncompliance That Are Firmly and Consistently Enforced.

In recent years, "alternative incarceration" and supervision programs have emerged. These include urine testing and hair analysis, house arrest with electronic monitoring, day reporting centers with group therapies, intensive boot camps, and sure and rapid incarceration for noncompliance in treatment. All have have had some success although the successes are minimal and mixed. In addition, the long-term effectiveness of these approaches have shown varied results. Some program approaches (e.g. boot camps and intensive supervision) are effective mainly at reducing incarceration costs, however, when subsequent reincarcerations and violations are factored into the costs, these programs lose some of their appeal. Recidivism evaluations of boot camps have indicated that a few do actually reduce expected recidivism by modest rates while others have little or no effect. Boot camps that show reductions in recidivism are characterized by high levels of therapeutic interventions (i.e., cognitive-behavioral therapy) in support of the typical discipline and work characteristic of boot camps. Ineffective boot camps are characterized solely by focusing on discipline and work.

Studies conducted by the U. S. Government Accounting Office in 1993 have actually shown that certain types of alternative incarceration and intensive supervision actually cost more than simple incarceration. However, if the client clearly understands that they will be held accountable for their actions through a systematic behavioral method, reductions in recidivism occur. Failures on intensive supervision can be predicted by unemployment and high numbers of prior convictions (Jones, 1995).

3. Specific Cognitive Skills Approaches Addressing Criminal Thinking, Thought Processes, and Decision-Making.

With the merging of cognitive therapies with behavioral strategies in the early 1980s, various specialized approaches have emerged focused on specific offender problems. Cognitive skills programs are typically run like an educational class and focus on narrowly defined issues like making rational decisions or managing finances and finding employment (Husband & Platt, 1993). Some problems have emerged with the format in that offender dropouts, transfers, and absences make classes smaller and more like groups. In addition, many of the approaches require a minimal reading level that squeezes too many offenders out. In addition, outcome studies on cognitive skills development are based on short time periods after treatment (typically less than one year). Also touted as a cognitive skills approach are certain "relapse prevention" models that teach abusers and offenders to recognize the behavioral signs and conditions when they typically relapse. These programs also teach coping skills to offenders and substance abusers. Then, the reasoning goes, the offender has the choice to choose an alternative to relapse. Relapse prevention certainly has its proponents, however, the approach unfortunately has very little data supporting its effectiveness. The earliest forms of relapse prevention were purely behavioral in nature and did show some beneficial effect on relapse (Little, 1996). Many of the cognitive skills programs in use today also appear to be based on behavioristic concepts of "self-efficacy" and "skills-deficits" proposed by relapse prevention proponents in the 1970s and 80s.

Some of the current relapse prevention methods appear to require substantial intellectual functioning levels of the participants and one of the best known relapse prevention models has virtually no outcome data on offending substance abusers. The first author of this monograph has devised a pure cognitive-behavioral relapse prevention system based upon classic cognitive-behavioral interventions for substance abusers (Little, 1997).

One other issue should be addressed here. Initial excitement over educational based cognitive skills programs stemmed from relatively short-term (6-months) recidivism data and low costs of the intervention. More recent research has shown the long-term effects of these programs is dubious. Related to this issue is the idea that all cognitive-skills programs are identical (this is an important issue because many institutions base their decisions on cost alone). It is simply not true that all all cognitive skills programming is identical. For example, Leiber and Mawhorr (1995) evaluated the effects of the *Youth Crossroads Program* (a 16 group session cognitive-skills program) on one-year recidivism rates. Results showed that treatment completers and treatment dropouts both had much higher recidivism rates than two separate control groups.

4. Cognitive-Behavioral Strategies Including Rational Emotive Therapy, Rational Behavior Therapy, or Moral Reconation Therapy®.

Some studies have shown that Rational Emotive Therapy and Rational Behavior Therapy are effective with offenders when done in their "pure" method. Unfortunately, these two methods rely on the therapist to maintain the "pure" RET or RBT perspective. Few practitioners of these two methods in criminal justice settings or substance abuse treatment centers apply the method in the same fashion. It is common for programs using these methods to "mix methods" in that they attempt to use RBT or RET while being a client-centered therapist. One of the basic problems seen in using these methods in programs is that there is no single RBT or RET client workbook. Thus, programs are inconsistent in their application of the approach.

Moral Reconation Therapy (MRT®) was first implemented

in 1985 in a prison-based drug therapeutic community by this monograph's authors (Little & Robinson, 1988). MRT attempts to create and maintain a therapeutic community environment within its group meetings. MRT has specific treatment workbooks depending on the client's facility, however, all MRT practitioners perform the method in the same fashion using the same sequence of exercises and therapeutic procedures. Because MRT primarily involves group work, wherein clients bring to group specific drawings and exercises, MRT can be done with clients with low reading levels. The system adjusts to each individual's needs and clients work at their own pace in "open-ended" groups. MRT is now in use in hundreds of different offender treatment sites in about 30 states and is used as substance abuse treatment in several state correctional departments. Results from MRT outcome data has shown that it reduces participants' recidivism rates by one-third to one-half during the 7-year time period immediately after offenders' release. Outcome data on MRT has been collected on thousands of participants. A recent review of MRT results cited 46 published reports on the method (Little, Robinson, Burnette, & Swan, 1996). In addition, massive independent evaluations have taken place within the Oklahoma Department of Corrections and the Delaware Department of Corrections with smaller reports coming from other states. The results of these studies are consistent. The cognitive-behavioral approach of MRT significantly reduces expected recidivism and cuts disciplinary infractions by 25% to 55%.

TAKING AIM AT ANTISOCIAL THINK-ING & BEHAVIOR: SPECIFIC HINTS

Various theorists have identified the most frequent thinking and behavioral errors by antisocials. Below we have listed some of the most frequently reported issues in thinking and behavior along with specific suggestions to cope with them:

1. *ASPDs tend to have a criminal or negative self-identity.* That is, they think of themselves as a "druggie," a "gangster," a "rebel," or "tough." Effective programming must reverse this image by having clients perform more positive activities and expose them to role

models who they respect and who have a more positive identity. It is essential that group and individual programming strive to develop and maintain positive identity.

2. *ASPDs tend to think that others cannot be trusted and are dishonest just as they are.* Programs must show the ASPD clients, through their own behavior and the way they run their program, that they can be trusted and are honest. Honesty, trust, and consistency must be held in high respect by the program itself.

3. *ASPDs are impulsive and lack internal controls.* Effective programs must require that clients maintain positive behavior indefinitely and earn privileges through sustained behavior. Time based rewards are necessary for this to occur and frustration tolerance builds as clients have to "wait" for rewards. A behavioristic approach is very useful to achieve this.

4. *Self-awareness is poor in ASPDs.* Programs must show the client how it is their behavior that gets them into trouble, not that they get caught. ASPDs must learn to take responsibility for their actions and those that they have hurt. They must also come to realize what they have to do to reverse their choices in life.

5. *ASPDs are often apathetic and indifferent.* Programs must force (through rules) clients to behave "as if" they cared about others. ASPDs do not see that they have to change, so programs must reward them for changing. You must show th*em the wisdom of change and some conformity to rules.* Over time and experience they will receive some rewards for the behavior and it will become more ingrained.

6. *ASPDs tend to have negative peers and associates.* Clients must come to understand and accept that the people they most trust *can't be trusted* and those they trust the least can be trusted. Their peers and associates tend to lead them into trouble and the price of "loyalty" to their friends is pain and suffering. Programs must show clients the path to developing more positive peers and relationships.

> *ASPDs tend to think that others cannot be trusted and are dishonest just as they are. ...ASPDs don't like to deal with real life.*

> **Programs must show the ASPD clients, through their own behavior and the way they run their program, that they can be trusted and are honest. Honesty, trust, and consistency must be held in high respect by the program itself.**

7. *ASPDs don't like to deal with real life.* ASPDs want what they want instantly. They don't like to work for it and would just as soon take it from someone else. Program rules must stress the importance of real-life activities and show clients the wisdom of following rules and being consistent in handling the constant problems that emerge in day-to-day life.

8. *Be on the ASPDs' side.* ASPDs are accustomed to being against society, programs, and rules and having others oppose them. Tell them you are on their side and show them you want them to be successful. In your occupation you should wish for their success.

9. *Reward their successes in the program and reward them for following the rules.* Establish a group procedure for making a big deal out of client accomplishments — whether it is the giving of a small, tangible reward or a round of applause.

10. *Maintain a positive peer pressure.* Hold group participants accountable when they don't discuss issues (call it nonconcern) or act disinterested. Verbally praise clients for making statements wherein they show concern for others (not remorse). Don't allow negative peer comments to go unchallenged.

11. *Have clients assess themselves as if they are assessing another client.* Have them list their strengths and weaknesses and make suggestions for improvements. ASPDs like picking others apart and are often quite good at it. If you can get them to pick apart someone "who acts and thinks just like they do," they will eventually begin to change.

12. *Be blunt and confrontive in a manner that lets them know you care (you are on their side).* Many counselors find being blunt difficult, but understand that clients won't break and that they usually appreciate the bluntness.

BATTERERS & ASPD

In recent years the issue of domestic violence and battering has become more important and noticeable. About 5% of men batter women and a much smaller number of women batter. Most batterers programs are based upon the assumption that battering is the man's attempt to gain power and control over a woman. This assumption has been validated by research from as early as 1980 (National Institute of Justice, 1995). Alcohol use is typically present in battering cases, but researchers and treatment providers are quick to correctly emphasize that battering is not caused by alcohol. Data indicates that 76% of batterers self-report alcohol problems and 65% show the alcohol dependence diagnosis. Over 70% show a drug dependence diagnosis. The use of drugs and alcohol by batterers parallels that of ASPDs.

Research on batterers' personality and behavioral characteristics has uncovered three distinct subtypes or clusters of perpetrators of domestic violence. One subtype, sometimes called the *Typical Batterer* or the *Second Cluster*, tends to batter only when drinking and shows remorse. Approximately 25% of batterers tend to fall into this cluster. It is likely that this subgroup does not represent ASPD diagnoses.

The so-called *Antisocial Batterer*, also referred to as the *First Cluster*, tends to be angry, jealous, shows little remorse, uses severe forms of violence, and abuses drugs and or alcohol. This subgroup tends to have a criminal record in addition to the battering and is, in all probability, ASPD.

The *Third Cluster*, sometimes called the *Sociopathic Batterer*, is the most violent of the three groups and perpetrates violent acts frequently and to various persons. This subgroup tends to report abuse as a child, abuses drugs and alcohol, shows little jealousy and anger, no remorse, and has a long and varied criminal record. Persons in this grouping also have a high probability of being ASPD.

Research on batterers has also focused on personality disorders. In a paper presented at the American Society of Criminology in 1986, Hamberger and Hastings reported that 80% of wife assaulters have diagnosable personality disorders. Hart, Dutton, & Newlove (1993) found that 90% of batterers were diagnosable with personality disorders based on personality tests. Dutton and Starzomski (1994) assessed differences in diagnoses in groups of batterers referred to treatment from criminal justice as compared to self-referred batterers. Their study showed that 66% of the court referred batterers showed ASPD while 54% of the self-referred showed ASPD. In addition, 66% of the court referred batterers also met the criteria for Aggressive-Sadistic Personality Disorder as compared to 78% of the self-referred.

Many traditional treatments have completely failed to impact battering and little outcome research has been generated on the newer power and control models. In 1995 the authors (Little & Robinson, 1995) modified the MRT® model for use on batterers since research showed that a majority of batterers who are forced into treatment have ASPD. Little data is available on outcome at this time. However, data from a large Montana implementation showed that 41% of all participants showed a prior chemical dependency diagnosis with an additional 9% having another mental health diagnosis. Other client data indicated that over 80% had prior misdemeanor arrests, 43% showed prior felony arrests, and 44% were repeat batterers.

SUMMARY

Robert Hare's (1993) text on ASPDs, *Without Conscience*, states the essential problems with treating ASPDs. ***ASPD clients simply don't believe that they have a problem and see no reason to change.*** "They never look back with regret or forward with concern. They perceive themselves as superior beings in a dog-eat-dog world in which others are competitors for limited power and resources" (p. 195). Hare goes on to say why many treatments may actually make ASPDs worse. Hare tells us that many inappropriate programs and interventions inadvertently provide the ASPD with excuses and a better way of manipulating and conning others for their personal gain. Programs treating ASPD clients should be cautious in not providing them with any excuses whether it be chemical dependency, abused childhoods, inability to read and write, or inability to get a good, high-paying job. The focus must be taken from *their* feelings and wishes to their behavior and the effects of their behavior on others. Perhaps this is why the only effective treatments for the antisocial personality to date are cognitive-behavioral, behavioral, or specific cognitive skills interventions. Such programs avoid discussing client feelings, trying to raise the self-esteem of people who already have inflated esteem, or identifying some cause in their childhood showing how the client isn't responsible for their behavior. Slowly, treatment providers are converging on focused treatment techniques that address these concerns. Finally, since research has shown us that we can reduce expected failures (as measured by recidivism) through cognitive-behavioral and purely behavioristic methods, we need to acknowledge that some treatment does beneficially impact the ASPD.

REFERENCES

Bootzin, R. R., & Acocella, J. R. (1984) *Abnormal psychology: current perspectives.* New York: Random House.

Brooner, R. K., Schmidt, C. W., Felch, L. J., & Bigelow, G. E. (1992) Antisocial behavior of intravenous drug abusers: implications for diagnosis of antisocial personality disorder. *American Journal of Psychiatry*, 149, 482-487.

Bureau of Justice Statistics (1992a) *Drugs and crime facts: 1992.* Washington, DC: U.S. Department of Justice.

Bureau of Justice Statistics (1992b) *Drugs, crime, and the justice system.* Washington, DC: U. S. Department of Justice.

Bursten, B. (1972) The manipulative personality. *Archives of General Psychiatry*, 26, 318-321.

Chapman, A. H. (1967) *Textbook of clinical psychiatry.* New York: Lippincott.

Cleckley, H. (1964) The *mask of sanity.* St Louis: Mosby.

Corsini, R. (Ed.) (1973) *Current psychotherapies.* Itasca, IL: Peacock Pubs.

Craig, R. J. (1988) A psychometric study of the prevalence of DSM-III Personality Disorders among treated opiate addicts. *The International Journal of the Addictions*, 23, 115-124.

Craig, R. J. (1993) Contemporary trends in substance abuse. *Professional Psychology: Research & Practice*, 24, 182-189.

Davidson, G. M. (1956) The syndrome of oligothymia psychopathy. *Journal of Nervous & Mental Disorders*, 124, 156-162.

Dutton, & Starzomski (1994) Psychological differences between court-referred and self-referred wife assaulters. *Criminal Justice and Behavior*, 21, 203-222.

Eliany, M., & Rush, B. (1992) *How effective are alcohol and other drug prevention and treatment programs?* Canada: Health and Welfare Canada.

Farabee, D., Nelson, R., & Spence, R. (1993) Psychosocial profiles of criminal justice- and noncriminal justice-referred substance abusers in treatment. *Criminal Justice and Behavior*, 1993, 20, 336-346.

Foon, A. E. (1988) The effectiveness of drinking-driving treatment programs: a critical review. *The International Journal of the Addictions*, 23, 151-174.

Freedman, A. M., Kaplan, H. I., & Saddock, B. J. (1976) *Comprehensive textbook of psychiatry/II.* Baltimore: Williams & Wilkins.

Freucht, T. E., Stephens, R. C., & Walker, M. L. (1994) Drug use among juvenile arrestees: a comparison of self-report, urinalysis, and hair assay. *The Journal of Drug Issues*, 24, 99-116.

Gendreau, P., & Ross, R. R. (1987) Revivification of rehabilitation: evidence from the 1980s. *Justice Quarterly*, 3, 349-407.

Gibbons, D. C. (1970) *Delinquent behavior.* Englewood Cliffs, NJ: Prentice-Hall.

Gilliland, B. E., James, R. K., & Bowman, J. T. (1994) *Theories and strategies in counseling and psychotherapy.* Boston: Allyn and Bacon.

Gorski, T. T. (1993) *The chemically dependent criminal offender: recovery and relapse prevention in the criminal justice system.* Independence, MO: Herald House.

Gunderson, J. (1983) DSM-III diagnosis of personality disorders. In J. Frosch (Ed.) *Current perspectives on personality disorders* (pp. 20-39). Washington, DC: American Psychiatric Press.

Guze, S. B., & Goodwin, D. W., & Crane, J. B. (1969) Criminality and psychiatric disorders. *Archives of General Psychiatry*, 205, 583-591.

Hare, R. D. (1980) A research scale for the assessment of psychopathy in criminal populations. *Personality and Individual Differences*, 1, 111-117.

Hare, R. D. (1993) *Without conscience: the disturbing world of psychopaths among us.* NY: Pocket Books.

Hare, R. D., Hart, S. D., & Harpur, T. J. (1991) Psychopathy and the DSM-IV criteria for Antisocial Personality Disorder. *Journal of Abnormal Psychology*, 100, 391-398.

Hart, S. D., Dutton, & Newlove (1993) The prevalence of personality disorders among wife assaulters. *Journal of Personality Disorders*, 7, 329-341.

Hemphill, J. F., Hart, S. D., & Hare, R. D. (1994) Psychopathy and substance use. *Journal of Personality Disorders*, 8, 169-180.

Hesselbrock, M. N., Meyer, R. E., & Keener, J. J. (1985) Psychopathology in hospitalized alcoholics. *Archives of General Psychiatry*, 42, 1050-1055.

Hilsenroth, M. J., Hibbard, S. R., Nash, M. R., & Handler, L. (1993) A Rorschach study of narcissism, defense, and aggression in Borderline, Narcissistic, and Cluster C Personality Disorders. *Journal of Personality Assessment*, 60, 346-361.

Hindman, J. (1988) New insight into adult and juvenile sexual offenders. *Community Safety Quarterly*, 1, 3.

Husband, S. D., & Platt, J. J. (1993) The cognitive skills component in substance abuse treatment in correctional settings: a brief review. *Journal of Drug Issues*, 42, 31-41.

Jones, M. (1995) Predictors of success and failure of intensive probation supervision. *American Journal of Criminal Justice*, 19, 239-255.

Jovanovic, M. D., Svrakic, D., & Tosevski, D. L. (1993) Personality disorders: a model for conceptual approach and classification. *American Journal of Psychotherapy*, 47, 558-571.

Kessler, R. C., McGonagle, K. A., Zhao, S., Nelson, C. B., Hughes, M., Eshleman, S., Wittchen, H., & Kendler, K. S. (1994) Lifetime and 12-month prevalence of DSM-III-R psychiatric disorders in the United States. *Archives of General Psychiatry*, 51, 8-19.

Khantzian, E. J., & Treece, C. (1985) DSM-III psychiatric diagnosis of narcotic addicts. *Archives of General Psychiatry*, 442, 1067-1071.

Kleinman, P. H., Miller, A. B., Millman, R. B., Woody, G. E., Todd, T., Kemp, J., & Lipton, D. S. (1990) Psychopathology among cocaine abusers entering treatment. *Journal of Nervous and Mental Disease*, 178, 442-447.

Kolb, L. C. (1968) *Noyes' modern clinical psychiatry*. Philadelphia: W. B.. Saunders.

Lawson, G. W., Ellis, D. C., & Rivers, P. C. (1984) *Essentials of chemical dependency counseling*. Rockville, MD: Aspen Publishers.

Leiber, M. J., & Mawhorr, T. L. (1995) Evaluating the use of cognitive skills training and employment with delinquent youth. *Journal of Criminal Justice*, 23, 127-141.

Leukefeld, C. G., & Tims, F. M. (1992) *Drug abuse treatment in prisons and jails*. Rockville, MD: NIDA.

Lipton, D. S., Falkin, G. P., & Wexler, H. A. (1990) *Correctional drug abuse treatment in the United States: an overview*. Rockville, MD: NIDA.

Little, G. L. (1992) *Cognitive behavioral treatments applied to substance abusers: a monograph*. Memphis, TN: Eagle Wing Books.

Little, G. L. (1997) *Psychopharmacology: Basics For Counselors.* Memphis: Advanced Training Associates.

Little, G. L. (1997) *Staying Quit: A Cognitive-Behavioral Workbook for Relapse Prevention.* Memphis: Advanced Training Associates.

Little, G. L. (1996) Relapse Prevention: an overview. *Focus,* 2.

Little, G. L., & Robinson, K. D. (1995) *Bringing peace to relationships: an MRT® educational workbook.* Memphis: Eagle Wing Books.

Little, G., & Robinson, K. D. (1994) Cost effectiveness, rehabilitation potential, and safety of intermediate sanctions: mixed results. *Cognitive-Behavioral Treatment Review,* 3 (1), 4-7.

Little, G. L., & Robinson, K. D. (1989) Effects of Moral Reconation Therapy on moral reasoning, life purpose, and recidivism among drug and alcohol offenders. *Psychological Reports,* 64, 83-90.

Little, G. L., & Robinson, K. D. (1988) Moral Reconation Therapy: a systematic step-by-step treatment system for treatment resistant clients. *Psychological Reports,* 62, 135-151.

Little, G. L., & Robinson, K. D. (1990) Reducing recidivism by changing how inmates think: the systematic approach of Moral Reconation Therapy. *American Jails,* 4(3), 12-16.

Little, G. L., Robinson, K. D., & Burnette, K. D. (1992) Cognitive-behavioral treatment for offenders. The *IARCA Journal on Community Corrections,* September, 5-9.

Little, G. L., Robinson, K. D., & Burnette, K. D. (1993) Cognitive behavioral treatment of felony drug offenders: a five-year recidivism report. *Psychological Reports,* 73, 1089-1090.

Little, G. L., Robinson, K. D., Burnette, K. B., & Swan, E. S. (1996) Review of outcome data with MRT®: seven year recidivism results. *Cognitive-Behavioral Treatment Review,* 5, (1), 1-7.

MacKay, J. R. (1986) Psychopathy and pathological narcissism: a descriptive and psychodynamic formulation on the Antisocial Personality Disorder. *Journal of Offender Counseling, Services & Rehabilitation*, 11, 77-94.

Magura, S., Kang, S. Y., & Shapiro, J. L. (1995) Measuring cocaine use by hair analysis among criminally-involved youth. *The Journal of Drug Issues*, 25, 683-701.

Malow, R. M., West, J. A., Williams, J. L., & Sutker, P. B. (1989) Personality Disorders classification and symptoms in cocaine and opioid addicts. *Journal of Consulting and Clinical Psychology*, 57, 765-767.

Mason, D. A., & Frick, P. J. (1994) The heritability of antisocial behavior: a meta-analysis of twin and adoption studies. *Journal of Psychopathology and Behavioral Assessment*, 16, 301-323.

Mervis, J. (1986) Rehabilitation: can it work now? APA *Monitor*, September, 14.

Morgan, R. L., Eagle, S. G., Esser, E., & Roth, W. M. (1993) Moral reasoning in adjucated youth residing at a boy's ranch. *Journal of Correctional Education*, 44, 62-66.

Myers, D. G. (1992) *Psychology*. New York: Worth.

National Institute of Justice (1995) *Report on the violence against women research strategic planning workshop*. Washington: NIJ.

Norden, K. A., Klein, D. N., Donaldson, S., Pepper, C. N., & Klein, L. M. (1995) Reports of the early home environment in DSM-III-R personality disorders. *Journal of Personality Disorders*, 9, 213-223.

O'Boyle, M. (1993) Personality disorder and multiple substance dependence. *Journal of Personality Disorders*, 7, 342-347.

Overholser, W., & Owens, D. J. (1961) The "psychopath": some legal and treatment aspects. *Journal of Social Therapy*, 7, 127-134.

Page, J. D. (1971) *Psychopathology*. Chicago: Aldine - Atherton.

Palmer, T. (1993) *Programmatic and nonprogrammatic aspects of successful intervention*. LaCrosse, WI: IARCA.

Penick, E., Powell, J. Othmer, E., et. al. (1984) Subtyping alcoholics by co-existing psychiatric syndromes. In: *Longitudinal research in alcoholism*. D. W. Goodwin, R. T. Van Dusen, S. A. Mednick (Eds.) Hingham, Mass.: Kluwer-Nijhoff.

Pennington, L. A., & Berg, I. A. (1954) *An introduction to clinical psychology*. New York: Ronald Press.

Phelps, L., & McClintock, K. (1994) Papa and peers: a biosocial approach to conduct disorder. *Journal of Psychopathology and Behavioral Assessment*, 16, 53-67.

Pugh, D. N. (1993) The effects of problem-solving ability and locus of control on prisoner adjustment. *International Journal of Offender Therapy and Comparative Criminology*, 163-176.

Ratliff, M. S. (1993) Classification of male substance-abusing incarcerated offenders and treatment indications: a cluster-analytic study. Unpublished dissertation, Nashville: Vanderbilt University.

Reid, W. H. (1985) The antisocial personality: a review. *Hospital and Community Psychiatry*, 36, 831-837.

Resnick, H. S., Foy, D. W., Donahoe, C. P., & Miller, E. N. (1989) Antisocial behavior and Post-Traumatic Stress Disorder in Vietnam veterans. *Journal of Clinical Psychology*, 45, 860-866.

Robbins, L. N. (1966) *Deviant children grown up: a sociological and psychiatric study of sociopathic personality*. Baltimore: Williams & Wilkins.

Robbins, L., & Regier, D. (Eds.) (1991) *Psychiatric disorders in America*. New York: Free Press.

Robinson, K. D., & Little, G. L. (1989) Drugs and criminal justice issues. In A. J. Giannini & A. E. Slaby (Eds.), *Drugs of abuse.* Oradell, NJ: Medical Economics Books. Pp. 427-440.

Rosenthal, D. (1970) *Genetic theory and abnormal behavior.* New York: McGraw Hill.

Rounsaville, B. J., & Kleber, H. D. (1985) Untreated opiate addicts: how do they differ from those seeking treatment? *Archives of General Psychiatry,* 42, 1072-1077.

Samenow, S. E. (1984) *Inside the criminal mind.* New York: Times Books.

Shea, M. T., Widiger, T. A., & Klein, M. H. (1992) Comorbidity of Personality Disorders and Depression: implications for treatment. *Journal of Consulting and Clinical Psychology,* 60, 857-868.

Sherman, L. W. (1993) Defiance, deterrence, and irrelevance: a theory of the criminal sanction. *Journal of Research in Crime & Delinquency,* 30, 445-473.

Smith, C., & Thornberry, T. P. (1995) The relationship between childhood maltreatment and adolescent involvement in delinquency. *Criminology,* 33, 451-477.

Snyder, H. N., & Sickmund, M. (1995) *Juvenile offenders and victims: a national report.* Pittsburgh: National Center for Juvenile Justice.

Spiecker, B. (1988) Psychopathy: the incapacity to have moral emotions. *Journal of Moral Education,* 17, 98-104.

Swan, N. (1993) Researchers probe which comes first: drug abuse or antisocial behavior. *NIDA Notes,* May/June, 6-7.

Tobey, L. H., & Bruhn, A. R. (1992) Early memories and the criminally dangerous. *Journal of Personality Assessment,* 59, 137-152.

Tolan, P., & Guerra, N. (1994) *What works in reducing adolescent violence: an empirical review of the field.* Boulder, CO: Center for the Study and Prevention of Violence.

Van Kamen, W. B., & Loeber, R. (1994) Are fluctuations in delinquent activities related to the onset and offset in juvenile illegal drug use and drug dealing? *The Journal of Drug Issues,* 24, 9-24.

Veneziano, C., & Veneziano, L. (1992) The relationship between deterrence and moral reasoning. *Criminal Justice Review,* 17, 209-217.

Widiger, T., Frances, A., Spitzer, R., & Williams, J. (1988) The DSM-III-R personality disorders: an overview. *American Journal of Psychiatry,* 145, 786-795.

Wolman, B. B. (Ed.) (1965) *Handbook of clinical psychology.* New York: McGraw Hill.

Woody, G. E., McClellan, T., Luborsky, L., & O'Brien, C. P. (1985) Sociopathy and psychotherapy outcome. *Archives of General Psychiatry,* 42, 1081-1086.

ABOUT THE AUTHORS

Dr. Kenneth D. Robinson received his Doctor of Education Degree in Educational Psychology and Counseling and a Master of Science Degree in Psychology from the University of Memphis. He is the President of Correctional Counseling, Inc. and is the co-developer of Moral Reconation Therapy (MRT®). He is Executive Editor of *Cognitive Behavioral Treatment Review* and was Executive Editor of *ACRIM News* in 1993-1994 and Associate Editor of *Recovery Times* in 1990-1992. He was Director of Clinical Services and Director of the Crisis Stabilization Unit for Midtown Mental Health Center in Memphis, Tennessee. He also worked in Mental Health Services for the Shelby County Correction Center from 1975-1987 and worked for a year with Project CERCE at the State Regional Prison in Memphis. Dr. Robinson conducts frequent training and workshops in MRT® throughout the United States and Puerto Rico. He has published and presented numerous professional articles in the areas of psychopharmacology and mental health. He is co-author of all of the MRT® treatment materials and other books including *How To Escape Your Prison, Your Inner Enemy, Filling The Inner Void, Character Development, Family Support, Job Readiness, Understanding & Treating The Antisocial Substance Abuser, Parenting and Family Values, Discovering Life & Liberty in the Pursuit of Happiness, Coping With Anger*, and *Bringing Peace To Relationships*.

Dr. Gregory L. Little received his Doctor of Education Degree in Counseling and a Master of Science Degree in Psychology from the University of Memphis. He is a trainer for Advanced Training Associates and Correctional Counseling, Inc. and is Editor of *Cognitive Behavioral Treatment Review*. He served as Editor of *ACRIM News* in 1993-1994 and was the Editor of *Recovery Times* in 1990-1992. Dr. Little taught in Shelby State Community College's Substance Abuse Counseling Certification Program from 1990-1993 and was the Director of the Drug & Alcohol Treatment Programs at the Shelby County Correction Center for 10 years where he was the co-developer of MRT®. He also worked at Project CERCE and was a consultant at FCI-Memphis for three years. He has published and presented several hundred articles in the areas of substance abuse treatment, psychopharmacology, and mental health and conducts MRT® training in the United States and Puerto Rico. Dr. Little is author of the books *The Archetype Experience* (1984), *People of the Web* (1990), *Grand Illusions* (1994), *Staying Quit: A Cognitive-Behavioral Relapse Prevention Guide* (1997), and *Psychopharmacology: Basics for Counselors* (1997). He is also co-author of all of the MRT® treatment materials and other books including *How To Escape Your Prison, Your Inner Enemy, Filling The Inner Void, Character Development, Family Support, Job Readiness, Parenting and Family Values, Understanding & Treating The Antisocial Substance Abuser, Discovering Life & Liberty in the Pursuit of Happiness, Coping With Anger,* and *Bringing Peace To Relationships*.